An Analysis of

Émile Durkheim's

On Suicide

Robert Easthope

Published by Macat International Ltd
24:13 Coda Centre, 189 Munster Road, London SW6 6AW.

Distributed exclusively by Routledge
2 Park Square, Milton Park, Abingdon, Oxon OX14 4RN
711 Third Avenue, New York, NY 10017, USA

Routledge is an imprint of the Taylor & Francis Group, an informa business

www.macat.com
info@macat.com

Cataloguing in Publication Data
A catalogue record for this book is available from the British Library.
Library of Congress Cataloguing-in-Publication Data is available upon request.
Cover illustration: Capucine Deslouis

ISBN 978-1-912303-72-4 (hardback)
ISBN 978-1-912127-25-2 (paperback)
ISBN 978-1-912282-60-9 (e-book)

Notice
The information in this book is designed to orientate readers of the work under analysis,
to elucidate and contextualise its key ideas and themes, and to aid in the development
of critical thinking skills. It is not meant to be used, nor should it be used, as a
substitute for original thinking or in place of original writing or research. References and
notes are provided for informational purposes and their presence does not constitute
endorsement of the information or opinions therein. This book is presented solely for
educational purposes. It is sold on the understanding that the publisher is not engaged
to provide any scholarly advice. The publisher has made every effort to ensure that
this book is accurate and up-to-date, but makes no warranties or representations with
regard to the completeness or reliability of the information it contains. The information
and the opinions provided herein are not guaranteed or warranted to produce particular
results and may not be suitable for students of every ability. The publisher shall not be
liable for any loss, damage or disruption arising from any errors or omissions, or from
the use of this book, including, but not limited to, special, incidental, consequential or
other damages caused, or alleged to have been caused, directly or indirectly, by the
information contained within.

CONTENTS

THE MACAT LIBRARY

The Macat Library is a series of unique academic explorations of seminal works in the humanities and social sciences – books and papers that have had a significant and widely recognised impact on their disciplines. It has been created to serve as much more than just a summary of what lies between the covers of a great book. It illuminates and explores the influences on, ideas of, and impact of that book. Our goal is to offer a learning resource that encourages critical thinking and fosters a better, deeper understanding of important ideas.

Each publication is divided into three Sections: Influences, Ideas, and Impact. Each Section has four Modules. These explore every important facet of the work, and the responses to it.

This Section-Module structure makes a Macat Library book easy to use, but it has another important feature. Because each Macat book is written to the same format, it is possible (and encouraged!) to cross-reference multiple Macat books along the same lines of inquiry or research. This allows the reader to open up interesting interdisciplinary pathways.

To further aid your reading, lists of glossary terms and people mentioned are included at the end of this book (these are indicated by an asterisk [*] throughout) – as well as a list of works cited.

Macat has worked with the University of Cambridge to identify the elements of critical thinking and understand the ways in which six different skills combine to enable effective thinking.
Three allow us to fully understand a problem; three more give us the tools to solve it. Together, these six skills make up the **PACIER** model of critical thinking. They are:

ANALYSIS – understanding how an argument is built
EVALUATION – exploring the strengths and weaknesses of an argument
INTERPRETATION – understanding issues of meaning

CREATIVE THINKING – coming up with new ideas and fresh connections
PROBLEM-SOLVING – producing strong solutions
REASONING – creating strong arguments

To find out more, visit **WWW.MACAT.COM.**

CRITICAL THINKING AND *ON SUICIDE*

Primary critical thinking skill: INTERPRETATION
Secondary critical thinking skill: ANALYSIS

Emile Durkheim's 1897 *On Suicide* is widely recognized as one of the foundational classic texts of sociology. It is also one that shows the degree to which strong interpretative skills can often provide the bedrock for high-level analysis.

Durkheim's aim was to analyse the nature of suicide in the context of society itself – examining it not just as an individual decision, but one in which different social factors played important roles. In order to do this, it was vital that he both define and classify suicide into subtypes – kinds of suicide with different causal factors at play. From his research, Durkheim identifed four broad types of suicide: egoistic (from a sense of not-belonging), altruistic (from a sense that group goals far outweigh individual well-being), anomic (from lack of moral or social direction), and fatalistic (in response to excessive discipline or oppression). These definitions opened the way for Durkheim to pursue a close social analysis examining how each type related to different social contexts.

While his study is in certain ways dated, it remains classic precisely because it helped define the methodology of sociology itself – in which interpretative skills remain central.

ABOUT THE AUTHOR OF THE ORIGINAL WORK

Émile Durkheim was a key figure in the establishment and development of sociology as a recognized science. Born into an Orthodox Jewish family in eastern France in 1858, he was academically gifted and moved to Paris to study. There, after the possible suicide of a close friend, Durkheim became interested in the bonds that link the individual to society—and what happens when those bonds break.

This interest became the focus of his scientific life. Durkheim spent years gathering data on suicides, looking for patterns, and creating a scientific framework to analyze the rates. He was the first person to bring a coherent sociological approach to such social issues, and fought hard to establish sociology as a distinct science separate from psychology. He died in Paris in 1917 at the age of 59.

ABOUT THE AUTHOR OF THE ANALYSIS

Robert Easthope holds an MSc in race and postcolonial studies from the London School of Economics.

ABOUT MACAT

GREAT WORKS FOR CRITICAL THINKING

Macat is focused on making the ideas of the world's great thinkers accessible and comprehensible to everybody, everywhere, in ways that promote the development of enhanced critical thinking skills.

It works with leading academics from the world's top universities to produce new analyses that focus on the ideas and the impact of the most influential works ever written across a wide variety of academic disciplines. Each of the works that sit at the heart of its growing library is an enduring example of great thinking. But by setting them in context – and looking at the influences that shaped their authors, as well as the responses they provoked – Macat encourages readers to look at these classics and game-changers with fresh eyes. Readers learn to think, engage and challenge their ideas, rather than simply accepting them.

'Macat offers an amazing first-of-its-kind tool for interdisciplinary learning and research. Its focus on works that transformed their disciplines and its rigorous approach, drawing on the world's leading experts and educational institutions, opens up a world-class education to anyone.'

Andreas Schleicher
Director for Education and Skills, Organisation for Economic
Co-operation and Development

'Macat is taking on some of the major challenges in university education … They have drawn together a strong team of active academics who are producing teaching materials that are novel in the breadth of their approach.'

Prof Lord Broers,
former Vice-Chancellor of the University of Cambridge

'The Macat vision is exceptionally exciting. It focuses upon new modes of learning which analyse and explain seminal texts which have profoundly influenced world thinking and so social and economic development. It promotes the kind of critical thinking which is essential for any society and economy.
This is the learning of the future.'

Rt Hon Charles Clarke, former UK Secretary of State for Education

'The Macat analyses provide immediate access to the critical conversation surrounding the books that have shaped their respective discipline, which will make them an invaluable resource to all of those, students and teachers, working in the field.'

Professor William Tronzo, University of California at San Diego

WAYS IN TO THE TEXT

KEY POINTS

- The French sociologist Émile Durkheim (1858–1917) is considered to be one of the founders of sociology,* the study of human society.

- *On Suicide*, published in 1897, gives a powerful sociological explanation of why people choose to take their own lives. Durkheim argues that higher rates of suicide in some societies may in fact be the result of social forces, rather than simply caused by individual problems.

- Durkheim's approach has inspired and challenged readers ever since, and remains the cornerstone of nearly all sociological investigations of suicide.

Who Was Émile Durkheim?

Émile Durkheim, author of *On Suicide*, was born in 1858 in Lorraine, France, to parents of modest means. His father was the local Jewish rabbi* (religious teacher), and both his grandfather and his great-grandfather had also been rabbis. Durkheim began his education at a religious school, but decided not to go down the same path as his father, and instead focused his brilliant intellect on establishing the value of a young academic discipline called sociology.

Sociology is the study of our social world's structure and development, and Durkheim was particularly interested in the ways individuals are connected to society. He became one of sociology's key figures, making significant contributions to our understanding of morality, religion, and suicide. His work helped to establish sociology in French universities, and several modern schools of sociology still take inspiration from his texts. *The Division of Labor* (1893), *The Elementary Forms of Religious Life* (1912), and *On Suicide* (1897) are all essential reading for sociology students and are still analyzed in many modern academic works.

Durkheim's career as a university professor began in 1887 when he was appointed to a teaching post at the University of Bordeaux. During his time there he established France's first-ever course on sociology and founded *L'Année Sociologique*, France's first journal of social science. In 1897 he published *On Suicide*. Durkheim meant this to be a demonstration of sociological analysis, as well as proof that his idea of a "social fact" was coherent and useful. Significantly though, he was also continuing the Durkheim family tradition of providing guidance on moral issues—looking for the causes of and solutions to one of society's biggest issues.

In 1902, and with the success of *On Suicide* behind him, Durkheim was appointed to the University of Paris (more commonly referred to as the Sorbonne*). This was a significant personal achievement. According to his nephew Marcel Mauss,* who would himself become a sociologist, Durkheim's sociological approach to studying moral issues had faced massive opposition from the philosophers at the Sorbonne.[1] This opposition went back to the time when Durkheim had mounted the oral defense of his own doctoral thesis at the university, and the negative feeling that had been shown towards him then had prevented him from making an earlier return to the capital. Once Durkheim did arrive, however, he managed to become both important and influential. One of his critics complained that he was "the regent of the Sorbonne," and that even the philosophers there were "dominated by his authority."[2] The French philosopher Xavier

Léon* suggested that this power had a lot to do with Durkheim's appearance and manner. He had, according to Léon, the "face and body of an ascetic" and his voice "expressed an ardent faith which … burned to mold and force the convictions of his hearers."[3] Durkheim's power within the university was widely criticized, but many agreed with the argument that "his ends were noble … [and] all the steps he took … had the single objective of the interest of science and the community."[4]

Sadly, many of the new generation of "Durkheimian" intellectuals who belonged to this community were killed in World War I,* and Durkheim's own son, André, was among them. Durkheim's initial response to this personal tragedy was to throw himself even more into the war effort. Eventually, however, it proved too much: "I have," he said to one of his friends in 1917, "the sensation of speaking to you about men and things with the detachment of someone who has already left the world."[5] For a man who had always acted with great passion this was a very bad sign. Émile Durkheim died later that year, on November 15, 1917, aged just 59.

What Does *On Suicide* Say?

In *On Suicide* Durkheim gives the first coherent sociological explanation of suicide. We often think of suicide as a private and individual decision. And we might wonder whether a mental disorder is to blame. But Durkheim argues that there is a definite social element to suicide. He bases this argument on a study of suicide rates—that is, the number of people of a certain group who commit suicide. Durkheim finds that different social groups have different suicide rates, and that those rates remain about the same each year. For example, by the late nineteenth century scholars knew that more Protestants* committed suicide each year than Roman Catholics,* and that military men killed themselves more often than civilians. Durkheim believes these suicide rates are good examples of what he calls "social facts"*—a concept he had developed in his previous works. By "social facts," he is referring to phenomena that we should study as if they are "realities external to the individual."[6]

At the time Durkheim was writing, some people were suggesting that nonsocial factors such as psychology, climate, heredity, and the idea of "race" could explain the differences between suicide rates. Durkheim disagrees. He thinks that because suicides are social facts, then only social factors can explain them. He goes on to describe four social conditions that push us toward suicide, conditions that change over time and whose importance varies from society to society. He calls these conditions egoism,* altruism,* anomie,* and fatalism:*

- Egoism describes conditions where the connections between society and individuals are weak. Durkheim argues that these weaker links lead to higher numbers of suicides.
- Altruism describes conditions where the links between society and the individual are too strong. The military needs to build a collective mentality for war, which includes soldiers obeying orders unthinkingly. This inevitably means individuals lose their sense of self and, as a result, seemingly trivial matters can be enough to provoke suicide. Hence there are higher suicide rates among the military.
- Anomie, can be understood as the result of low moral regulation within society. Durkheim thinks this can explain the high number of suicides after economic crises. Such crises disrupt people's moral compass, causing them to want more from life than they can achieve. Durkheim believes that anomie is endemic in modern society.
- Fatalism is a term used by Durkheim to describe the opposite state to anomie, one in which there is an excess of moral regulation. He believes that fatalism explains the suicides of people living in oppressive conditions such as slavery. He also believes, however, that fatalism is much less common than anomie, and therefore only uses a footnote within *On Suicide* to discuss it.

On Suicide argues that the level of social integration and regulation within a society determines its suicide rates. According to Durkheim, these "forces" can even explain *individual* cases of suicide. This suggests that it is not personal troubles such as bankruptcy, bereavement or shame that cause suicide, but rather the wider problems that affect society in general. This argument was controversial and challenging, and it remains so for readers of the text today.

On Suicide is still the key contribution from the discipline of sociology to the study of suicide. It has provided a framework for many later studies, and plenty of inspiration for others. For example, a 2011 review of the subject categorized all work on suicide as either pre-Durkheim, Durkheim, or post-Durkheim.[7] And most post-Durkheim research still tries to clarify, update, or challenge Durkheim's original theory.

Why Does *On Suicide* Matter?

On Suicide is regarded as one of the great classic texts of sociology. No introductory sociology textbook would fail to mention it, and most sociology students will read excerpts during their studies. But why is this? What is it about this analysis of suicide in nineteenth-century Europe that has made it so important to sociology today?

One factor explaining its significance is that Durkheim was not only interested in individual suicide cases—he was also linking personal troubles to the structural changes happening around him, which included increasing specialization in the workplace, the growth of cities, and the increasing influence of capitalism.* Those changes continue to affect us today, meaning that Durkheim's text still has a powerful message, and still speaks to the *causes* of suicide. It can even now help us to understand our relationship to the society around us.

But *On Suicide* also tells us something deeper about sociology. According to sociology professor Michael Overington,* "classic" sociology texts such as *On Suicide* do three things: they illustrate what sociology is; they promote a way to do it; and they tell us "what sociologists stand for."[8] *On Suicide* shows that when we look at individuals' actions en masse, we can see new patterns. It combines sophisticated reasoning with statistical evidence. And it shows how, right from its beginnings, sociology was concerned with problems that affect people in tangible, sometimes tragic, ways.

Written over a hundred years ago, *On Suicide* makes use of fairly unreliable data and rather basic statistical analysis by today's standards. But nevertheless, it does show what can be achieved even with limited data when they are paired with logical but *creative* reasoning. The text manages to rise above its empirical* limitations (that is, it rises above problems with the data themselves and the analysis of those data) to provide a framework that is still useful today.

In short, *On Suicide* is a powerful testament to the strengths and virtues of our sociological imagination. And as such, it has a direct and continuing relevance to the study of suicide.

NOTES

1   Steven Lukes, *Émile Durkheim: His Life and Work* (Harmondsworth: Penguin, 1975), 301.

2   Agathon, as quoted in Lukes, *Émile Durkheim*, 373.

3   Léon, as quoted in Lukes, *Émile Durkheim*, 370.

4   Bourgin, as quoted in Lukes, *Émile Durkheim*, 377.

5   Davy, as quoted in Lukes, *Émile Durkheim*, 559.

6   Émile Durkheim, *On Suicide*, trans. J. A. Spaulding and G. Simpson (London: Routledge, 2002), xxxvi.

7   Matt Wray, Cynthia Colen, and Bernice Pescosolido. "The Sociology of Suicide." *Annual Review of Sociology* 37 (2011): 505–28.

8   Michael A. Overington, "A Rhetorical Appreciation of a Sociological Classic: Durkheim's 'Suicide,'" *Canadian Journal of Sociology* 6, no. 4 (1981): 457.

SECTION 1
INFLUENCES

MODULE 1
THE AUTHOR AND THE HISTORICAL CONTEXT

KEY POINTS

- *On Suicide* (1897) is one of the great classic works of sociology,* which is the study of our social world's structure and development.

- Émile Durkheim wrote *On Suicide* to show how sociology should be done, and why it is worth doing.

- The text was written at a time when many commentators were worried about the negative effects on people's lives of industrialization*—the shift from manual labor to new machinery to get work done.

Why Read This Text?

Émile Durkheim's *On Suicide* was first published in 1897. The text gives a powerful sociological explanation of why people choose to take their own lives—that is, to commit suicide. Durkheim argues that the number of people who commit suicide—the suicide rate—differs across societies, because in some of those societies there are stronger social forces pushing people toward death. This is an approach that has inspired sociologists ever since, and scholars still use Durkheim's ideas to explain suicide—a phenomenon as complex as it is tragic. Indeed, most work on suicide can still be categorized and understood best in terms of its relation to Durkheim's position. This means that *On Suicide* is still sociology's primary contribution to this area of study.

On Suicide is essential reading for those who are interested in suicide, but it also has a wider importance. Durkheim was not only trying to explain suicide, he was also trying to demonstrate what

> **❝** Émile Durkheim taught the modern world how to think about suicide. **❞**
>
> Richard Sennet, introduction to Durkheim, *On Suicide*

sociology as a discipline is, how it is separate from psychology*—the study of the mind and its functions, and how it affects behavior—and why his approach made more sense than those of his rivals. What is known as Durkheimian sociology has had a powerful influence on the development of the discipline, and *On Suicide* is therefore an important text for anyone interested in the foundations of sociological thought.

Author's Life

Émile Durkheim was born in Lorraine, France on April 15, 1858. His upbringing as the youngest child of an Orthodox* (strict) Jewish family was modest, despite his father holding an important position in the community as the local religious leader, known as the rabbi*—a role eight generations of the family had filled. Durkheim himself would also follow in this long tradition of learning, but not by studying at a yeshiva* (a Jewish religious school). Instead he worked hard to gain a place at the prestigious École Normale Supérieure* in Paris, in 1879. Here the atmosphere was one of lively debate and exchange, and Durkheim's generation was particularly brilliant, producing large numbers of important academics and politicians. While the most famous of his peers was probably the philosopher Henri Bergson* (who was in the year above Durkheim), for Durkheim himself the most influential may well have been a young man called Victor Hommay.*

Hommay became a close friend of Durkheim, and after graduation the two kept in contact during their time teaching at *lycées* (French provincial sixth-form colleges). Taking such a post was standard practice for the graduates, but Hommay found the hardships, particularly the lack of social life, difficult. When Hommay fell, or quite possibly jumped, out of a second-floor window, the young Durkheim was confronted for the first time with the phenomenon of suicide that he would later write so insightfully about.[1]

Author's Background

Before the publication of *On Suicide* in 1897, as far back as the end of the eighteenth century, there was a widespread feeling in Europe that suicide was a growing social issue. Through the nineteenth century, it became one of the most discussed social problems, with a growing mass of literature and material devoted to it. Like Durkheim, many commentators across the political spectrum believed that this was to do with industrialization, a process whereby newly invented labor-saving machines were replacing humans in the workforce. This was clearly changing society in dramatic and permanent ways.[2] Durkheim's first book, *The Division of Labor in Society* (1893), dealt with this in a direct manner. It argued that while these changes were indeed far-reaching, they would *change* rather than *destroy* society's moral foundation. It is possible to interpret *On Suicide* as an exploration of how the negative effects of industrialization can be understood and countered.

But not all commentators were convinced that rising suicide rates *were* connected to these large-scale social changes. Some important figures argued that most (or indeed all) suicides were related to mental illness; other commentators thought that factors such as climate and "race" were crucial; and there were sociologists who argued that psychological phenomena such as imitation*—somebody copying someone else's behavior—could explain things. All these ideas were in flux at the time Durkheim began writing *On Suicide*.

NOTES

1   Steven Lukes, Émile Durkheim: His Life and Work (Harmondsworth: Penguin, 1975), 44–51.

2   Anthony Giddens, "The Suicide Problem in French Sociology," *British Journal of Sociology* 16, no. 1 (1965): 3–18.

MODULE 2
ACADEMIC CONTEXT

KEY POINTS

- Sociology* was not an established discipline when Durkheim was writing *On Suicide*, and he wanted to change this situation.

- The rising suicide rates in Europe at the time had attracted attention from many scholars and social commentators alike.

- Through *On Suicide*, Durkheim planned to show how sociology could help us understand suicide.

The Work in its Context

At the time that Émile Durkheim published *On Suicide*, in 1897, many scholars in Europe were already describing and examining the steady rise in suicides—a trend many thought was a symptom of a greater moral decline. They saw this moral decline as developing when society in general showed lower levels of morality, often associated with rising crime rates and less interest in religion. The breakdown of traditional society and the introduction of industrialization* through a mechanized manufacturing industry that threatened many people's jobs was the most common explanation for these trends. But investigators also tended to assume that mental illness was involved in most suicides. Other factors, some that fitted with this idea of a moral decline, had also been put forward. These included climate, "race," and the social effect of imitation.[1]

The discussion had led to the discovery of certain statistical links related to suicide. It was known, for example, that suicide rates varied with age, sex, and marital status. There were also higher suicide rates in

> ❝ Instead of contenting himself with metaphysical reflection on social themes … [the sociologist] must take as the object of his research groups of facts clearly circumscribed, capable of ready definition, with definite limits, and adhere strictly to them. ❞
>
> Émile Durkheim, *On Suicide*

Protestant* populations than in Roman Catholic* ones. Urban populations appeared to be more at risk than rural ones. And finally, the likelihood of suicide seemed to vary according to the time of the year, the day of the week, and even the hour of the day. Economic recessions had been shown to be associated with sharp rises in suicides, while populations in a constant state of economic depression—meaning the poor—had lower rates than people in liberal occupations such as teaching and medicine.[2] By the time Durkheim came to the topic, a large amount of information already existed that needed to be organized into a system before coherent explanations for suicide could be found. Durkheim saw this as the perfect task to demonstrate the usefulness of sociology.

Overview of the Field

At the beginning of Durkheim's career, sociology was not a well-established academic discipline. The writings of Auguste Comte* (the philosopher who first used the word "sociology" in its modern sense) had lost respectability and there had never even been a sociology professor in France. Philosophers "knew in general and quite vaguely that Comte had proposed this word to designate social science: they were unanimous in finding it bizarre and unwarranted."[3] Durkheim, though, saw something worthwhile in the term, and as he began preparing his doctoral dissertation on the relationship between individuals and social cohesion, he decided that the best way forward was to treat the subject sociologically.[4]

21

In Durkheim's view, the key figures in the history of sociology had been philosophers rather than sociologists, examining society for no other reason than to support their rather grand ideas. He found something much more relevant in a book about animal societies written by the French thinker Alfred Espinas.* Durkheim praised the way Espinas tried to derive laws from careful observation of the facts, and he was clearly influenced by the idea that states of animal consciousness could only be explained by the nature of the group.[5] By 1885, Durkheim was convinced that "sociology has now emerged from the heroic age… Let it establish itself, become organized, draw up its program and specify its method."[6] Durkheim set out to publish books with that aim in mind. *On Suicide* was one of the final pieces in this plan.

Academic Influences

Durkheim's *On Suicide* was—and still is—of interest, mainly because of the theoretical framework Durkheim used to make sense of the empirical* patterns (meaning those patterns provable by observation or experience) displayed by suicide rates. This was due in part to his previous intellectual encounters with a number of sociological thinkers. Among these, Comte, Émile Boutroux,* Herbert Spencer,* and Ferdinand Tönnies* stand out. Boutroux was one of Durkheim's teachers at the École Normale Supérieure.* He taught Durkheim that each branch of science should use its own principles to make explanations, a rule that *On Suicide* follows very closely.[7] Comte also held this view, and contributed, like Spencer and Tönnies, to Durkheim's ideas about how individuals are connected to society, and how that relationship evolves and varies in different societies. The four particular social conditions that Durkheim associates with high suicide rates—egoism,* anomie,* altruism,* and fatalism*—derive from, and build on, these ideas, which appear in his first text, *The Division of Labor in Society* (1893).

- Egoism is an undesirably low level of social integration.
- Anomie is a lack of social regulation.
- Altruism is an undesirably high level of social integration.
- Fatalism is an undesirably high level of social regulation.

Another influence on Durkheim were those writers sometimes grouped together under the term "moral statisticians."* Durkheim inherits the idea that statistical data can tell us about the moral status of society from probably the most important of these, Adolphe Quetelet,* one of the first scholars to use statistics to study the social world. Durkheim criticizes his ideas about voluntary death in *On Suicide*.

NOTES

1   Anthony Giddens, "The Suicide Problem in French Sociology," *British Journal of Sociology* 16, no. 1 (1965): 3–18.

2   Giddens, "Suicide Problem," 3–18.

3   Alfred Espinas, as quoted in Steven Lukes, *Émile Durkheim: His Life and Work* (Harmondsworth: Penguin, 1975), 66.

4   Lukes, Émile Durkheim, 66.

5   Lukes, Émile Durkheim, 84.

6   Durkheim, as quoted in Lukes, Émile Durkheim, 85

7   Lukes, Émile Durkheim, 57–58.

THE PROBLEM

KEY POINTS

- Scholars had found patterns in suicide rates, but they were struggling to explain them.

- Some scholars, such as the statistician and sociologist* Gabriel Tarde,* thought that the key to understanding social phenomena was by looking at individual, psychological factors such as imitation.*

- Durkheim wanted to show that social facts*—that is, the things in society, such as suicide rates, that constrain our behavior and drive us to act in certain ways—could only be explained by examining social causes.

Core Question

Émile Durkheim's *On Suicide* has a single question at its heart: what determines a group's suicide rate? This is an important question because if we know the answer, then we might be able to stop people finding themselves in situations where suicide seems an attractive option. For Durkheim, the question was also significant for a number of other reasons.

First, throughout his career Durkheim was interested in what links individuals to society. He believed that suicide was essentially the severing of this link. He seems to have thought that if he could explain why suicide happens, then the bonds that normally link us to society would be clearer. By investigating the abnormal, he hoped to find out about the normal. Durkheim also believed that examining a *group* phenomenon such as the overall suicide rate, as opposed to looking at *individual* cases of suicide, forces us to pay attention to the social causes

> " If instead of seeing here only particular events, isolated one from another, each of which ought to be considered separately, we consider all the suicides committed in a given society over a given period of time, we shall observe that the total we obtain is not a simple sum of independent units, a collective whole, but that it constitutes a new fact, in itself and *sui generis* [that is, unique], which has its own unity and individuality, and so its own nature; and that, moreover, this nature is eminently social. "
> Émile Durkheim, *On Suicide*

of a particular phenomenon. A single case might be explained by an individual's *particular* circumstances, but the rate at which people kill themselves (given that it is constant for certain groups) requires us to look for causes that are *general* in their society.

Durkheim was not alone in asking the question. Previous scholars had been intrigued by the same problem and had suggested various factors to explain why people in some groups or locations are more prone to suicide than others. What sets Durkheim's investigation apart, however, is the *way* in which he approaches the issue. As the British sociologist Anthony Giddens* points out, Durkheim brings a coherent sociological approach to the problem that allows him to explore the meaning of, and relationship between, various empirical* correlations (that is, links that can be proved through the use of real data).[1] Durkheim was the first to do this, and the way he did it has influenced scholars ever since.

The Participants

On Suicide was written while its author battled to establish and shape sociology in France. Durkheim wanted to show how sociology—the study of our social world's structure and development—was distinct from psychology*—the study of the mind and its functions, and how it affects behavior. This much is clear in the argument he directs against the ideas of the statistician and sociologist Gabriel Tarde.

Tarde was the director of the French Ministry of Justice's criminal statistics bureau, and arguably France's most important sociologist at the time Durkheim was writing *On Suicide*. He provided a large amount of the raw data for Durkheim's suicide research. Tarde's own scholarly work spanned statistics, criminology*—the scientific study of crime and criminals—and sociology, and he had developed a distinctive approach to the last of these. This emphasized the importance of interactions between individuals and the power of imitation* and innovation* (the process of making something that is believed to be new) to explain social phenomena. These ideas put him on a collision course with Durkheim, who believed that social phenomena *must* be explained by social causes. Their debate was fierce. It has shaped our understanding of both men's ideas, and the way it unfolded set the course for how sociology has developed as a discipline.

A key participant in this debate was the French psychiatrist Jean-Étienne Esquirol,* whose book *Mental Maladies: A Treatise on Insanity* (1838) tried to classify all mental disorders. Esquirol believed that suicide was the result of mental illness and was often hereditary, meaning it was passed down through generations. Durkheim dealt with this argument in the first chapter of *On Suicide.*

The Contemporary Debate

Tarde had been involved in a debate with Durkheim ever since he had reviewed Durkheim's first major work, *The Division of Labor*, from 1893. Tarde believed that since society stems from individuals, sociology should be based on psychology. Following this principle, he had devised his own approach to sociology. This argued that we can recognize whether something is "social" by deciding whether it is "imitative": "Not everything that members of a society do is sociological… To breathe, digest, blink one's eyes … there is nothing social about such acts… But to talk to someone, pray to an idol, weave a piece of clothing, cut down a tree … those are social acts, for it is only the social man who would act in this way; without the example of the other men he has voluntarily or involuntarily copied since the cradle, he would not act thus. The common characteristic of social acts, indeed, is to be imitative."[2]

Durkheim, however, thought that basing sociology on a psychological concept such as imitation was a mistake. He wrote in *The Rules of Sociological Method* (1895): "[There] is between psychology and sociology the same break in continuity as there is between biology and the physical and chemical sciences. Consequently, every time a social phenomenon is directly explained by a psychological phenomenon, we may rest assured that explanation is false."[3]

Durkheim mentioned Tarde by name only once in *The Rules*— and that was in a footnote. Tarde, possibly insulted by this, fiercely criticized Durkheim's sociology in a series of articles. These set the scene for Durkheim's retaliation in *On Suicide,* a book that cannot be fully understood if read *only* as an investigation of suicide. *On Suicide* was a key part of Durkheim's argument for a sociology based on what he called social facts, such as the suicide rate.

NOTES

1   Anthony Giddens, "The Suicide Problem in French Sociology," *British Journal of Sociology* 16, no. 1 (1965): 5.

2   Tarde, as quoted in E. V. Vargas, B. Latour, B. Karsenti, F. Aït-Touati, and L. Salmon, "The Debate between Tarde and Durkheim," *Environment and Planning D: Society and Space* 26, no. 5 (2008): 763.

3   Durkheim, as quoted in Vargas et al., "The Debate," 763.

MODULE 4
THE AUTHOR'S CONTRIBUTION

KEY POINTS

- Durkheim argues that two social conditions in particular affect the suicide rate: social integration—the degree to which members of society are bound together; and social regulation—the control that social values and norms have over individuals.

- Durkheim's argument has defined sociology's* approach to suicide ever since.

- Durkheim constructed his framework by developing and adapting the theoretical concepts he had presented in his first text, *The Division of Labor in Society* (1893).

Author's Aims

On Suicide was part of Émile Durkheim's larger project to establish sociology as a reputable academic subject. Two years previously he had published his *Rules of Sociological Method* (1895) in book form, in which he argued that social facts* must be studied as if they are "realities external to the individual."[1] *On Suicide* was intended to demonstrate how this worked in practice—showing that sociology "deals with realities as definite and substantial as those of the psychologist or the biologist."[2] Durkheim thought that in suicide he had found a subject that was not only timely, but also ideally suited to this approach. He intended to use the study to show fellow sociologists the way forward, and to stake a claim for sociology's academic territory.

This explains the way in which Durkheim structures his text. First, he starts by discarding nonsocial causes of suicide. Then he moves on to find social causes by examining variations in suicide rates. Finally he

> ❝ [Leaving] aside so to speak the individual as individual, with his motives and his ideas, we shall ask directly what are the states of the different social *milieux* (religious faiths, family, political and professional groups, etc.) according to which suicide varies. Only then, coming back to individuals, shall we seek to know how these general causes are individualized to produce the homicidal effects involved. ❞
>
> Émile Durkheim, *On Suicide*

argues that these social causes are more important than the particular circumstances and motivations of individual cases. Given his stated aims, this is clearly an argument about the importance of social factors for an act that can on the surface seem wholly psychological, rather than purely an examination of the causes of suicide.

Durkheim arguably achieved his aims in *On Suicide*. The text helped to establish sociology in French universities, enthused future researchers about the potential of statistical data for understanding social problems, and showed why the concept of a social phenomenon always has a place in the sociologist's toolbox.

Approach

Perhaps the key idea of *On Suicide* is that explaining suicide rates is different from explaining individual suicides. According to Durkheim, the factors that determine which specific individuals within a group kill themselves are different from the factors that decide the (constant and distinct) rate of suicide for that group.

Durkheim was the first to stress this concept. As Durkheim put it, previous scholars had been known to look for "an inclination in the make-up of an individual, or at the very least of a significant class of individuals, which varies in intensity from one country to another and impels men directly to suicide."[3] Durkheim dismisses the contenders that were claimed to be responsible for this "inclination"—such as alcoholism or "nervous disorders"—because their rates do not correspond to the suicide rates: countries with high alcohol consumption do not necessarily have a high suicide rate, and neither do countries with high rates of mental illness. Durkheim takes a very different approach. Rather than look at the causes of *individual* suicides first, he tries to find the causes of differences in suicide *rates*. Why, for example, do more military men kill themselves than civilians? Why more Protestants* than Roman Catholics?* Why more unmarried men than married men?

Contribution in Context

One of *On Suicide*'s key themes is the importance of social factors, such as industrialization,* in suicide rates. Industrialization was the shift in society at that time towards using new machines to complete tasks in the working environment more quickly and efficiently than humans, and therefore threatening the livelihoods of a large number of people. So important and persuasive is this aspect of the text that commentators sometimes forget that neither the idea of treating suicide sociologically, nor the key statistical links it was based on, were original to Durkheim. This is a point the influential sociologist Anthony Giddens* made clear in 1965.[4] Giddens convincingly argues that the real originality of *On Suicide* lies in the way it puts preestablished empirical* links, provable through the use of data, into a coherent theoretical framework. In other words, Durkheim made sense of things.

It is also possible that it was Durkheim's Jewish background that drove his ambition to make sense of society's moral condition. Not only was his father, Moïse Durkheim, a rabbi,* so were his grandfather and great-grandfather. In all, eight generations of Durkheims had filled this role of spiritual and moral leader. The sociologists Eugen Schoenfeld* and Stjepan Meštrović* have suggested that, given that his father also had a strong interest in science, Émile Durkheim's career represented an attempt to combine his father's scientific ambitions with the tradition in his family of the men being moral guides in society.[5]

NOTES

1 Émile Durkheim, *On Suicide,* trans. J. A. Spaulding and G. Simpson (London: Routledge, 2002), xxxvi.

2 Durkheim, *On Suicide*, xxxvii.

3 Durkheim, *On Suicide*, 33.

4 Anthony Giddens, "The Suicide Problem in French Sociology," *British Journal of Sociology* 16, no. 1 (1965): 3–18.

5 Eugen Schoenfeld and Stjepan G. Meštrović, "Durkheim's Concept of Justice and its Relationship to Social Solidarity," *Sociological Analysis* 50, no. 2 (1989): 111–27.

SECTION 2
IDEAS

MAIN IDEAS

KEY POINTS

- Durkheim argued that suicide rates must be explained by social factors.

- He identified the key factors determining the suicide rate as social integration* and social regulation.* He called low social integration "egoism,"* high social integration "altruism,"* and low social regulation "anomie."*

- Durkheim made this argument in a patient, logical style that supported his claim that sociology* should be seen as a scientific discipline.

Key Themes

Two major ideas underpin Émile Durkheim's *On Suicide*. The first is that suicide rates cannot be explained by nonsocial factors. The second is that a group's suicide rate is determined by two social factors—namely, its level of social integration and its level of social (or moral) regulation. Durkheim wanted to show that sociological explanations can give a unique insight into actions which may at first seem very personal. He was also providing a practical example of the *method* of research he had first outlined in his earlier work, *The Rules of Sociological Method* (1895). *On Suicide* presents a theory of suicide and defends the way it was constructed—that is, through sociological methods.

Durkheim used the statistical variations in suicide rates across Europe to identify and describe three main social conditions that promote suicide: egoism, altruism, and anomie. (A fourth, fatalism,* is referred to in a footnote but not examined in detail.) These three conditions depend upon two variables: social integration and social

> ❝ When society is strongly integrated, it keeps individuals in a state of dependency, holding them to be in its service and consequently not permitting them to dispose of themselves. ❞
>
> Émile Durkheim, *On Suicide*

regulation. Social integration is the degree to which members of society are bound together; when it is low the result is egoism, and when it is high the result is altruism. Social regulation is the control that social values and norms have over individuals; low levels create anomie and high levels create fatalism. All four conditions can lead to high suicide rates, and in modern societies egoism and anomie are at abnormally high levels.

Exploring the Ideas

The first theme of *On Suicide* is the idea that there is only one possible place to look for the causes of suicide-rate variations—the social realm. At the time Durkheim was writing some people were suggesting that certain nonsocial factors might be the major cause of suicide. Durkheim examines these explanations one by one and argues that factors such as psychology,* heredity* (that is, the passing of characteristics, mental or physical, from generation to generation), "race," and climate fail to explain the differences in suicide rates. He reasons that this leaves us with only one possibility: suicide rates *must* have social causes.

The second theme of the text is Durkheim's identification of the three main social conditions that favor high suicide rates. He believed that social integration was a key variable for suicide.[1] He called low social integration "egoism," and argued that a well-integrated society provides a kind of safety net for those in trouble. If this is taken away, or if it never existed in the first place, people will be in more danger of opting for suicide. Durkheim believed that egoism encouraged suicide because in the modern world we are *social* beings. Our higher activities—art, science, morality—are given meaning by society and have no value without it. So if we lose contact with society, then these higher actions all begin to appear meaningless.

Altruism is the opposite of egoism. It occurs when society and the individual are bound together *too* closely. Durkheim uses this concept to explain why soldiers were more likely to commit suicide than civilians. He uses data to show that their high rates of suicide could not be explained by bachelorhood, alcohol consumption, or the difficulty of military life. Durkheim argues that people in the military become accustomed to obeying orders, resulting in a low sense of individualism and a low sense of self. This makes heroic self-sacrifices easier in the heat of battle, but because these men do not value the self, seemingly trivial matters can be enough to provoke suicide.

Durkheim called his third social condition "anomie," which is essentially a breakdown of moral order. To explain this concept, Durkheim uses the statistical link between suicide and economic crises. He argues that economic crises cause the suicide rate to rise because they disrupt moral regulation. In normal circumstances public opinion establishes what standard of living people can expect, given their occupation or class. This changes anyway over time, but the *collapse* of economic prosperity can lead to a breakdown of social order. Egoism also occurs when economic progress is no longer thought of as a means to an end. This is a problem because in such a situation there are no moral barriers to profit seeking, and because there is an almost infinite market desire that will never be satisfied. The result is a general condition of anomie in industry and commerce that makes economic crises all the more dangerous: "When one has no other aim than constantly going beyond the point that one has reached, how painful it is to be driven back!"[2]

It is important to understand that Durkheim believed these social conditions often occur in combination. This allows for a flexible and workable typology of suicide (that is, a classification of suicide according to type) that sociologists continue to use today.

Language and Expression

Durkheim generally writes in a careful, measured tone. When he describes the effect of egoism on the human psyche, however, he uses a powerful, almost poetic style, designed to convince the reader of his opinions. This was perhaps a conscious attempt to compensate for a lack of evidence about the way egoism, anomie, and altruism appear in individual cases. Because Durkheim could *show* his readers the numerical effect of integration and regulation on suicide rates, he presented those sections in analytical language. But because he had no *evidence* about how that effect actually worked, he changed his style.

It is also notable that throughout *On Suicide* Durkheim uses the language of collective forces and currents, though he never really defines the meaning of either "collective forces" or "currents." Using such terms was part of Durkheim's intention to establish the academic territory of sociology, but Steven Lukes,* a politics and sociology professor, suggests that "the polemic [that is, the strongly worded argument] and the metaphor [the use of figures of speech] tended to betray Durkheim into misrepresenting his own ideas, and into misleading himself and his readers as to their significance."[3] Lukes argues that while *On Suicide* is really about the "social preconditions for psychological health," Durkheim's language makes us think it is about the power of society.[4]

Despite this issue, Durkheim's three social conditions have entered the lexicon of social science. Anomie, in particular, has captured commentators' imagination over the years. Its characterization of capitalism's* effect on our psyche and mental health has proved influential.

NOTES

1   Émile Durkheim, *On Suicide*, trans. Robin Buss (London: Penguin Books, 2006), 224.

2   Durkheim, *On Suicide*, 281.

3   Steven Lukes, *Émile Durkheim: His Life and Work* (Harmondsworth: Penguin, 1975), 34.

4   Lukes, *Émile Durkheim*, 36.

SECONDARY IDEAS

KEY POINTS

- Durkheim uses suicide rates to demonstrate his concept of social facts* (of which the suicide rate is one). He also argues that the social factors that he thought determined the suicide rate are the fundamental reasons why people decide to kill themselves. People do not kill themselves because of personal circumstances.

- The social fact is still an important concept in sociology.* However, the idea that personal circumstances are not fundamentally important to suicide cases has become less influential.

- Durkheim was right to think that suicide rates are a persuasive example of social facts. His work shows how apparently personal decisions are affected by social conditions and it is still used to introduce students to sociology today.

Other Ideas

The concept of the social suicide rate is crucial to understanding Émile Durkheim's *On Suicide.* Rather than beginning his study by examining individual cases and then working out the causes of these suicides, Durkheim builds his theory by examining the number of suicides in a set place over a set period of time. He calls this the social suicide rate,* and uses it as an example of what he called a "social fact."

The social suicide rate is quite stable for each society. It changes only gradually year by year—unless a crisis (like a revolution or a war) causes a spike or a dip. Between societies, however, there seem to be significant differences. For instance, according to Durkheim's data

> ❝ [The] rate of suicide, while only showing slight
> annual variations, varies from society to society, being
> in some two, three, four or even more times what it
> is in others. It is thus, far more than mortality, specific
> to every social group and can be considered as a
> characteristic index for that society. ❞
>
> Émile Durkheim, *On Suicide*

there were 67 recorded suicides per million inhabitants in England for 1866–70, while in Sweden there were 85, in France 135, and in Denmark 277. A few years later, in 1874–78, the figures for the same countries were 69, 91, 160, and 255 respectively. There is clearly a stable pattern here. And if we think of suicide as purely a matter of individual circumstances, it is very difficult to explain these patterns. Why would individual circumstances occur with the roughly same frequency in the same countries each year?

Exploring the Ideas

Durkheim argues that the suicide *rate* gives a *numerical* value representing a society's "tendency to suicide." It shows that "every society is predisposed to supply a given number of voluntary deaths."[1] More radically, he claims that investigating the *causes* of a social suicide rate is different from investigating why certain individuals kill themselves. The two questions may be related, but they are not the same. It is the social suicide rate that Durkheim and sociologists in general are interested in.

The things that trigger one person's suicide may be quite particular to them, and will therefore not be general enough to affect a society's social suicide rate. So rather than investigating *all* the causes that push people to take their lives, it is only those which depend on "a particular state of social organization" that concern sociologists.[2] These are the ones general enough to affect the social suicide rate.

Durkheim writes that the obvious way to identify these general factors would be to observe and then categorize as many cases of suicide by sane individuals as possible. The resulting categories would correspond to certain social causes, which could then be investigated. However, this kind of information was not available at the time, and according to Durkheim, it might even be impossible to collect. So he decided to identify types of suicide by their *cause* rather than by their *form*, and he would only later try to confirm these types by referring to data on individual cases.

Given this strong focus on the social nature of suicide, it might be assumed that Durkheim has little to say about the causes of individual suicides, but this is not the case. After describing the three social conditions that seem to encourage high suicide rates, Durkheim argues that these represent the true causes of individual acts of suicide. Many different kinds of events and situations seem to cause individual cases of suicide (such as divorce or family tragedy), but it is really the way people *react* to these events that determines whether or not they take their own life—and the way they react depends on social conditions. So, according to Durkheim, a painful end to a relationship may or may not provoke someone to suicide. Whether it does or not "all depends on the intensity with which the suicidogenic causes [that is, the factors leading to suicide] have acted upon the individual."[3]

Overlooked

There is very little about *On Suicide* that has been completely overlooked. However, there has been a very important conversation about whether some aspects of the text *should* be overlooked. It is worthwhile examining the reasons that this conversation took place.

Sociologist Barclay DeLay Johnson* has suggested that altruism* (the undesirably high level of social integration) and fatalism* (the undesirably high level of social regulation) should be ignored because they are not really supported by Durkheim's analysis. His examples of altruism are primarily based on questionable European accounts of non-Western societies that do not mention suicide rates, and the cases of fatalism are inconsistent with Durkheim's own claim that suicide rates must be explained through social causes. Johnson also argues that egoism* (the undesirably low level of social integration) and anomie* (a lack of social regulation) are not as distinct as Durkheim presented them as being. Egoism implies a lack of social integration, and one of the negative effects of this is to undermine the socially given values and goals that give our life purpose. For some commentators this sounds exactly like the lack of moral regulation that Durkheim termed "anomie." If anomie is only one aspect of egoism, and all aspects of egoism increase or decrease together, than they must by definition coincide. Durkheim's theory is then reduced to just one law: "The more integrated (regulated) a society, group, or social condition is, the lower its suicide rate."[4]

Johnson's argument was first presented in 1965 and until recently has been influential. Various studies have overlooked Durkheim's discussion of altruism, anomie, and fatalism in favor of a greater emphasis on social integration's relationship with suicide. Social regulation might have been insignificant for understanding suicide trends in the past, but some of the major global variations in the suicide rates since the 1990s have challenged that perception. Areas that have experienced high suicide rates following periods of rapid social change, such as post-communist* Eastern Europe, South Korea, and now China, have made Durkheim's analysis of anomie (distinct from egoism in its ability to capture the effects of such transitions) seem increasingly relevant and there has been a rise in the number of studies examining this once-neglected aspect of *On Suicide*.

NOTES

1   Émile Durkheim, *On Suicide*, trans. Robin Buss (London: Penguin Books, 2006), 28.

2   Durkheim, *On Suicide*, 28.

3   Durkheim, *On Suicide*, 332.

4   Barclay D. Johnson, "Durkheim's One Cause of Suicide," *American Sociological Review* 30, no. 6 (1965): 886.

ACHIEVEMENT

KEY POINTS

- Durkheim succeeded in making sociology* a key academic discipline in France. His ideas about what sociology is, and how it functions, are still influential today, as is his framework for explaining suicide.

- Durkheim's preexisting ideas about social solidarity* (or the degree to which individuals are connected to social groups) and the way societies develop allowed him to approach the subject in a more coherent and insightful way than previous commentators.

- Durkheim may have over-exaggerated the power of his theory because of his ambitions for sociology. This led him to ignore what suicide means to individuals.

Assessing the Argument

Émile Durkheim's *On Suicide* played a major role in establishing sociology as a discipline in the French university system. It cemented Durkheim's reputation, enabling him to secure a place at the prestigious Parisian university La Sorbonne* as chair of education and sociology. It led to a large proportion of sociological work becoming less philosophical and more empirically* focused (that is, based on data and quantifiable evidence) in France and beyond. Durkheim's approach also gained a wide following in the United States.

However, Durkheim's ambition to prove the importance of sociology may have undermined his attempt to thoroughly explain suicide rates. He ignores what he terms "individual" factors (such as the meaning suicide has for those who actually take their own lives), and argues that his social causes offer a better explanation. But, as

> **❝** [No] writer before Durkheim had presented a consistent framework of sociological theory which could bring together the major empirical correlations which had already been established. **❞**
>
> Anthony Giddens, "The Suicide Problem in French Sociology"

politics and sociology professor Steven Lukes* has observed, "it is incoherent to claim that particular circumstances and 'motives and ideas' are irrelevant to the explanation of suicide (or indeed any human activity) … explaining suicide—and explaining suicide rates—must involve explaining why people commit it."[1]

It is fair to say that Durkheim did not complete the task of explaining suicide. However, the framework and the approach he developed showed that social factors are much more important than many people thought or expected. His methods also made it possible for generations of scholars to take up his ideas, test them, and, most significantly, expand upon them. This is a project that continues today.

Achievement in Context

It took Durkheim seven years to gather the data for *On Suicide*, and he mentions that his nephew (and pupil) Marcel Mauss* categorized some 26,000 suicide events on his own. It is hard to imagine now just how time consuming that would have been in a pre-computer age. In fact, given how much better (and quicker!) we are now at collecting and analyzing data, the continued importance of Durkheim's *On Suicide* may seem remarkable. However, even at the time he wrote the book it was not Durkheim's empirical findings that set the work apart. Rather, as British sociologist Anthony Giddens* emphasizes, it was the incorporation of these empirical findings into a coherent theoretical framework that was important.[2] Durkheim's study of suicide was the first to accomplish this, and the framework for study that he established helps us to find meaning in statistical patterns in suicide rates today.

Many of the problems Durkheim faced in collecting information about the meaning of suicide still confront researchers today. Obviously, we cannot ask people why they committed suicide, and notes written in times of emotional stress can have limited value. The similarities between attempted suicides and completed suicides are uncertain, so we must be careful about relying on testimonies from survivors. In this sense, today we still share many of the fundamental problems Durkheim was trying to overcome when he set out to write *On Suicide.*

Limitations

Durkheim built his entire argument on the observation that the rate of suicide varies between societies and sub-societies. Yet there are many who believe Durkheim mistakenly ignored just how different suicide is across societies. For these commentators, Durkheim failed to take into account the different *meanings* that suicide is given by individuals and cultures.

Scholars working outside Europe have stressed this limitation. For example, *Suicide and Justice: A Chinese Perspective* (2010), written by the Chinese professor Wu Fei,* suggests that Durkheim's account of suicide is misleading when applied to China.[3] On the basis of analyses of individual cases and the interpretations of them by people involved, Wu Fei argues that in the Chinese town where he conducted his research, suicide was not caused primarily by Durkheimian anomie (that is, the disruption or lack of social regulation), but instead by unjust treatment within the home and/or the local community.[4]

Wu Fei goes even further. He suggests that there is a fundamental problem with automatically applying a Durkheimian perspective in China, because suicide means something different in that culture. There is a concept of self that lies at the heart of *On Suicide* that does not fit Chinese understandings. Wu Fei argues that, according to Durkheim, human nature is universally composed of two parts—the individual, biologically determined part, and the social, externally determined part. When these two aspects are out of balance, then suicide becomes possible. But Wu Fei claims this is a culturally specific understanding. In China the family is much more important to selfhood than in the West. If we forget this, then we risk ignoring the role of domestic injustice in driving up Chinese suicide rates. The lesson is perhaps that we should always keep in mind just how complex suicide is.

NOTES

1   Steven Lukes, *Émile Durkheim: His Life and Work* (Harmondsworth: Penguin, 1975), 221.

2   Anthony Giddens, "The Suicide Problem in French Sociology," *British Journal of Sociology* 16, no. 1 (1965): 3–18.

3   Wu Fei, *Suicide and Justice: A Chinese Perspective* (London and New York: Routledge, 2010).

4   Wu Fei, *Suicide and Justice*, 69.

MODULE 8
PLACE IN THE AUTHOR'S WORK

KEY POINTS

- Throughout his academic career, Durkheim was interested in exploring the link between individuals and society. He thought he could understand this better by analyzing suicide because (according to him) suicide is what happens when there is something broken in this link.

- *On Suicide* demonstrates Durkheim's method for studying social issues.

- The text proved that his approach was insightful, and cemented his reputation in France. For most sociologists* today, it is the book that confirms Durkheim's genius.

Positioning

Émile Durkheim's *On Suicide* (1897) was his third major publication, preceded by *The Division of Labor in Society* (1893) and *The Rules of Sociological Method* (1895), both of which were written during a productive period at the University of Bordeaux. Like these earlier works, *On Suicide* provoked strong reactions both from critics and from those who appreciated his work.

Durkheim's academic engagement with suicide began long before his classic study was written. Nine years earlier, in 1888, he published an article on the topic, and even made it the focus of a one-year public course the following year. Durkheim worked on his ideas and collected statistics for the next seven years, helped in the latter task by former pupils and by his nephew, Marcel Mauss.* When he finally published his findings, the presentation itself was shaped by the struggles he was fighting on behalf of sociology generally. Durkheim clearly meant his

> **❝** The ideas presented in *Suicide* constitute a particularly forceful testimony to the fruitfulness of Durkheim's conception of sociological method. **❞**
>
> Anthony Giddens, *Capitalism and Modern Social Theory*

study to demonstrate the insights sociological* analysis can provide, and to prove that his concept of a social fact* was both coherent and useful. In looking for the causes of one of life's most fundamental troubles, he was also continuing the Durkheim family tradition of providing guidance in moral issues, his father, grandfather, and great-grandfather all having been rabbis.*

Integration

The degree to which Durkheim's work forms a coherent whole is strongly debated. The respected sociologist Jeffrey Alexander* has warned that these debates "are, inevitably, arguments about the most basic directions of sociological explanation and more general social thought."[1] Alexander himself has not shied away from the debate, claiming that Durkheim's work shows significant inconsistencies—not just between texts, but even within them. He also argues that just after *On Suicide* was written (but before it was published) Durkheim radically changed his own approach to sociology, resulting in greater cultural analysis, which was evident in his final major work, *The Elementary Forms of Religious Life* (1912).

The other side of the debate is well represented by another of today's influential social thinkers, Anthony Giddens,* whose 1978 introduction to Durkheim emphasizes the unity and coherence running from *The Division of Labor*, through *On Suicide*, and into *The Elementary Forms of Religious Life*.[2] The real relevance of this debate to students is that there is a tendency to refer to "early" and "late" Durkheim. The former includes *On Suicide*, and the latter mainly refers to Durkheim's work on religion, best represented in *The Elementary Forms of Religious Life.*

Significance

It would be difficult to argue that *On Suicide* established Durkheim's reputation. He had already produced a notable work in *The Division of Labor* (1893), and had published a number of articles in *L'Année sociologique*, the sociology journal he himself had founded. Nevertheless, it is a very significant work.

The sociologist Peter Hamilton* has argued that the key factor explaining the success of Durkheim and his followers ("Durkheimians") was his method.[3] Durkheim describes this in *The Rules of Sociological Method* (1895), but demonstrates its practical value in *On Suicide*. This is the text's real significance in relation to Durkheim's wider work.

On Suicide is the single Durkheim text most engaged with by scholars working on real-world problems today. His other works have inspired various ways of conducting sociology, but *On Suicide*'s specific predictions are still being tested. Unlike many of his contemporaries, Durkheim is not only discussed in terms of theory, or in terms of the history of the discipline, his practical propositions are still being challenged, adapted, and reinterpreted. Thanks to *On Suicide*, Durkheim is *directly* significant to sociology today.

NOTES

1   Jeffrey C. Alexander, "The Inner Development of Durkheim's Sociological Theory: From Early Writings to Maturity," in *The Cambridge Companion to Durkheim*, ed. Jeffrey C. Alexander and Phillip Smith (Cambridge: Cambridge University Press, 2005), 136.

2   Anthony Giddens, *Durkheim* (London: Fontana Press, 1978).

3   Peter Hamilton, "Introductory Essay: Emile Durkheim," in *Emile Durkheim: Critical Assessments*, ed. Peter Hamilton (London: Routledge, 1995), 8.

SECTION 3
IMPACT

THE FIRST RESPONSES

KEY POINTS

- Durkheim was criticized for trying to draw a distinction between studying suicide *rates* and studying suicide cases. He was also accused of romanticizing society and using imprecise language.

- Durkheim pointed out that the distinction between studying rates and studying cases was a methodological decision, not a philosophical stance.

- Durkheim's ideas might have caused less immediate controversy had he used a less dogmatic and aggressive style.

Criticism

Émile Durkheim's *On Suicide* was not met with universal approval when it was published in 1897. Perhaps the most powerful attack came from Gabriel Tarde,* director of the French Ministry of Justice's criminal statistics bureau. Tarde had developed his own approach to sociology* that emphasized the importance of interactions between individuals and the power of "imitation"* and "innovation"* to explain social facts.*

Tarde's debate with Durkheim was a long-running one, and many of their fundamental disagreements can be seen in Tarde's review of *On Suicide*. First, Tarde claimed that Durkheim failed to rule out the effect of imitation: Durkheim had claimed that if imitation was the cause of variations in suicide rates, then the map would show a series of circles with high rates in the center and lower rates on the outside. This was not the case. Tarde, however, claimed that the pattern

> ❝ It would have perhaps been more politic not to present things in this form. But what can I do? It is in my nature... But as you say, however basically simple the proposition may be, it is natural that it should be resisted to begin with. ❞
>
> Émile Durkheim, in a letter to Célestin Bouglé, 1897

Durkheim described would indeed occur if suicide were something new, but suicide is in fact an ancient phenomenon. Tarde believed that imitation was more useful for explaining the growth of language, art, and religion. So if Durkheim wanted to disprove Tarde's theory, he should, Tarde argued, show why imitation couldn't explain their growth.

Tarde went on to criticize Durkheim for using imprecise terminology and romanticizing the idea of society. He attacked Durkheim for his distinction between individual suicides and suicide rates, asking, "What is this social suicide rate which remains blissfully unaffected by the greater or lesser number of individual suicides?"[1] For Tarde, if imitation could cause an increase in the former (which Durkheim admitted), then it was nonsense to claim it couldn't affect the latter. It was, he said, "pure myth" that "the collective inclination exists above and apart from all of the individual inclinations to suicide."[2] It was on this source of disagreement that the two scholars would continue their debate.

Responses

The most penetrating of Tarde's criticisms concerned Durkheim's claim that explaining the suicide rate was a different project from explaining individual suicides. For him, the idea that collective tendencies are separate from individual tendencies was "pure myth."[3] Anticipating this attack, Durkheim had reiterated in *On Suicide* his view that society is not simply the sum of its parts: collective inclinations *can* be different from individual ones. Moreover, he argued, the fact that someone is part of a society does not mean that all of that society's thoughts and characteristics will be found within him or her. He argued that "of all the individual consciousnesses that make up the great mass of the nation, there is none with regard to which the collective current is not almost entirely external, since each of them only contains a fragment of it."[4] So the relationship between sociology and psychology* is similar to that between psychology and biology, or indeed to that between biology and chemistry. Just as an individual's psychology cannot be studied by analyzing single neurons, so collective phenomena, or social facts, cannot be studied through looking at individuals. In short, social facts are external to the individual.

Tarde thought this was a philosophical statement about reality, but Durkheim made it clear he meant it as a methodological one, stating: "It is due to the thoroughly engrained habit of applying to sociological matters the forms of philosophical thought that [our] preliminary definition has often been seen as a sort of philosophy of the social fact."[5] Tarde started with a philosophical view of social facts: to him, societies consist of individuals and therefore social facts must be internal to individuals. Durkheim, however, claimed to be trying to "delimit the field of enquiry as much as possible, [so as] not to flounder about in some exhaustive intuition."[6] He thought that to do otherwise would be to second-guess the findings of science.

Durkheim did not alter his view as a result of Tarde's criticism. Indeed, his second preface to *The Rules of Sociological Methods* (1901) convincingly refuted Tarde's criticisms of *On Suicide's* methodology.

Conflict and Consensus

Durkheim's fiercest critics, for whom suicide rates could *only* be explained by looking at individual situations or health, would never agree with him. Tarde and Durkheim never changed their opposing

'

views on the importance of individual factors for explaining social phenomena.

The famous British sociologist Anthony Giddens,* in his 1965 article "The Suicide Problem in French Sociology," has said that the debate depended on a false opposition between "the social" and "the individual." Durkheim dealt with the opposition by saying there was a methodological distinction between the study of suicide *rates* and the study of individual *cases*. Rates could be explained through "the social" by sociology, single cases through "the individual" by psychology. That separation continued long after Durkheim. This was what Durkheim wanted to achieve and, indeed, it helped provide an area of study that sociology could lay claim to. But his success had an unfortunate consequence: it restricted the application not only of his own concepts, but also of sociological analysis in general, to this one aspect of suicide. That, thought Giddens, was the major reason for the lack of progress he identified in suicidology up to 1965. The situation would change somewhat with the publication of Jack Douglas's* *The Social Meanings of Suicide* (1967), but it still remains true that sociologists have tended to follow Durkheim's lead in making suicide rates the focus of their studies.

NOTES

1   Tarde, as quoted in E. V. Vargas, B. Latour, B. Karsenti, F. Aït-Touati, and L. Salmon, "The Debate Between Tarde and Durkheim," *Environment and Planning D: Society and Space* 26, no. 5 (2008): 769.

2   Tarde, as quoted in Vargas et al., "The Debate," 770.

3   Tarde, as quoted in Vargas et al., "The Debate," 770.

4   Émile Durkheim, *On Suicide*, trans. Robin Buss (London: Penguin Books, 2006), 351.

5   Durkheim, as quoted in Vargas et al., "The Debate," 772.

6   Durkheim, as quoted in Vargas et al., "The Debate," 772.

THE EVOLVING DEBATE

KEY POINTS

- *On Suicide* has had a strong influence on sociology;* its ideas about suicide are still important, and its approach to how people do sociology has been taken up by modern, evidence-based sociologists.

- *On Suicide* can be seen as the forerunner of modern empirical sociology.*

- *On Suicide* showed how sociology could use quantitative* (or measurable) techniques to analyze patterns in suicide rates. Much of the sociological work done on suicide today has followed Durkheim's example.

Uses and Problems

Émile Durkheim's *On Suicide* has served as an inspiration for generations of followers. One of the first to take up Durkheim's project was the Frenchman Maurice Halbwachs,* who published a work called *Les causes du suicide* (*The Causes of Suicide*) in 1930. This work aimed to update and review Durkheim's findings. Halbwachs supported many of *On Suicide's* ideas, but he rejected Durkheim's four-way classification (egoism,* altruism,* anomie,* and fatalism*) in favor of a single cause—namely, a lack of social integration, which he renamed as "social isolation." Interestingly, Halbwachs also used this Durkheimian notion to account for the association between certain mental illnesses and suicide.

Other scholars who have used Durkheim's work have also found problems with his approach. American sociologist Jack Douglas* originally set out to build on Durkheim's work, but came to realize

> **❝** The widespread acceptance of sociology as an academic and scientific discipline is perhaps more attributable to Durkheim than any other sociologist, and *Suicide* is an essential source of that influence.**❞**
>
> Whitney Pope, *Durkheim's Suicide: A Classic Analyzed*

that there were a number of flaws in it. Durkheim's positivism*—the philosophy that regards only scientifically verifiable facts and laws as authoritative knowledge—led him to discount individual meanings and interpretations as something that could not be measured, and to assume that "the data spoke for themselves."[1] It is possible, therefore, that Durkheim could have made the data fit his own, preexisting interpretation of what suicide means. Another problem is that statistics on suicide may be culturally specific. For example, a particular community's willingness to classify a death as suicide might depend on whether suicide is socially acceptable within that community or not.

Douglas's work inspired another scholar, Max Atkinson,* to look for a more solid way to investigate such problems. Atkinson examined the process by which deaths become classified as suicides. He paid particular attention to coroners (that is, officials who investigate deaths that are out of the ordinary), and who require a plausible explanation or motive before they reach a verdict of suicide. According to Atkinson, such deaths must fit the coroner's own ideas about what kind of situations and types of death are typical of suicides. If they do not, then the death is not recorded as a suicide. Coroners' ideas about what constitutes a typical suicide seem to include the variables typically investigated by sociologists (i.e. divorce, depression, economic problems). There is a danger, therefore, that the statistical relationships between these variables and suicide are actually describing the indicators chosen by coroners to identify suicides.

Both Atkinson and Douglas showed where problems might arise in Durkheimian research into suicide. But it is important to note that neither of them was able to prove that these issues had *actually* affected the data being used.

Schools of Thought

Durkheim's influence on sociology and social thought is still recognized today. After Durkheim was given a position at the prestigious university La Sorbonne* in Paris in 1902, sociology emerged as a bone fide discipline in French academia. Many of those associated with Durkheim found careers in the government, while others continued in the academic world, making important contributions to a variety of subjects. In the interwar* years between World War I* and World War II*, however, the Durkheimians' own political successes gradually began to count against them. They became associated with the failures of France's Third Republic* (which ruled France between 1879 and 1940), and Durkheim became unfashionable.

Yet this did not mark the end of Durkheim's influence in France. Indeed, through his nephew, the sociologist and anthropologist Marcel Mauss,* and then his student, the anthropologist Claude Lévi-Strauss,* Durkheim's legacy continued to shape advances in social thought. His work also influenced the Swiss linguist Ferdinand de Saussure,* and he can be seen as a key inspiration for the structuralist* movement, as well as postmodernism* and deconstructivism.*

Structuralism is a school of thought that suggests that elements of human culture can only be understood in terms of their relations with other elements. These networks of relations constitute the "structure" of society. Postmodernism is a school of thought characterized by its rejection of the values and assumptions of (Western) modernity. In particular, postmodern philosophy has been skeptical about the power of reason. Deconstructivism is a form of critical analysis that draws attention to the instability of meaning.

Much of Durkheim's legacy draws on his later work. However, in the universities of 1930s America it was his early works (including *On Suicide*) that became influential. This was primarily due to the efforts of the sociologist Talcott Parsons.* Parsons devoted a large part of his 1937 work *The Structure of Social Action* to interpreting Durkheim's intellectual journey, making him one of the keystones of his own theory. Parsons's approach dominated mainstream American sociology until the 1960s and 1970s, and for a long time Durkheim's work became almost synonymous with Parsons's functionalist* sociology. Functionalism is the sociological perspective that analyses how social institutions contribute to the working of society as a whole. Unfortunately, when criticism of functionalism emerged in the mid-1970s, Durkheim's reputation suffered with it.

In Current Scholarship

Along with *The Rules of Sociological Method*, *On Suicide* played a key role in preparing the ground for modern empirical sociology, which is the dominant way of doing sociology today. This kind of sociology, which emphasizes the use of statistical techniques to analyze the results of tests or observations, does not always place much emphasis on its intellectual roots. It often prefers to draw authority from its method. Nevertheless, there is at its heart a "Durkheimian" approach that owes much to *On Suicide*.

Of course, *On Suicide*'s influence is most strong in sociological studies of suicide. Despite important interventions from interpretivist* scholars, such as Max Atkinson* (interpretivists focus on interpreting human behavior in context), the empirical* focus on suicide *rates* remains dominant. Since the 1980s there has been an emerging school of "Durkheimian" cultural sociologists.*[2] Members of this group of scholars, of whom Jeffrey Alexander* is a leading figure, emphasize the importance of Durkheim's final great work, *The Elementary Forms of Religious Life* (1912), rather than *On Suicide* or *The Division of Labor in*

Society (1893). They argue that "the center of gravity has decisively shifted from the early and middle Durkheim to the late," and that "[w]ith this Durkheim securely enthroned, the intellectual agenda has been altered for Durkheim's second one hundred years."[3] According to the cultural sociologists, we need to move on from Durkheim's concerns in *On Suicide*, and look toward the concepts he developed later, dealing with ritual* (defined sets of actions performed regularly) and the sacred* (things that are prohibited and set apart).

NOTES

1   Jack Douglas, *The Social Meanings of Suicide* (Princeton, NJ: Princeton University Press, 1967), 68.

2   Phillip Smith and Jeffrey C. Alexander, "Introduction: The New Durkheim," in *The Cambridge Companion to Durkheim*, ed. Jeffrey C. Alexander and Phillip Smith (Cambridge: Cambridge University Press, 2005).

3   Smith and Alexander, "New Durkheim," 31.

MODULE 11
IMPACT AND INFLUENCE TODAY

KEY POINTS

- *On Suicide* stands alongside German sociologist Max Weber's* *The Protestant Ethic and the Spirit of Capitalism* (1905) as one of sociology's* most defining works.

- *On Suicide* reminds us to pay attention to social factors when we try to explain social facts.*

- Critics favoring qualitative approaches* (measuring something according to quality rather than quantity) have pointed out that Durkheim's empirical* stance ignores the social meaning of suicide and the way in which that affects statistics about suicide.

Position

Émile Durkheim's *On Suicide* is considered a classic work of sociology. It is indeed a classic example of positivist* sociology, the sociology that regards only scientifically verifiable facts and laws as authoritative knowledge. And this type of sociology is a forerunner of the kind of quantitative* investigations of society that account for much of the sociological work done today. Yet *On Suicide* fails to meet many of the requirements of positivist sociology. Not only is the evidence Durkheim used to support his theories questionable, but it has even been argued that those theories may be untestable. So there is, as sociologist Michael Overington* has pointed out, a "contradiction" in holding it up as a positivist classic.[1] For Overington, this suggests that the reason for *On Suicide*'s status as *the* positivist classic actually lies in its ability to provide the arguments and the authority needed to justify a certain way of doing social science.

> **❝** It was the *issues* posed by Durkheim in a book which just happened to be on suicide, rather than the *phenomenon of suicide* itself, which has stimulated most of the sociological interest. **❞**
>
> Max Atkinson, *Suicide: Studies in the Social Organization of Sudden Death* (original italics)

However, *On Suicide* is not only important for positivists. Many people who do not think of sociology in these terms also regard it as a great work. The reason for its appeal must therefore be more general. Overington goes on to identify three key elements of the text that help it maintain its status as a "classic": it provides an illustration of what sociology is; it promotes one way to do it; and it tells us "what sociologists stand for."[2]

Interaction

When Durkheim wrote *On Suicide*, voluntary death was often thought to be primarily a psychological issue, and many scholars looked for an explanation in hereditary factors for characteristics that were passed down from generation to generation. Today, with advances in our understanding of biology, genetics* (the study of inherited characteristics), and the human brain, these ways of understanding and studying suicide may seem more likely to produce the breakthrough that will finally allow us to identify the people who might decide to kill themselves, as well as tell us *why* they choose to do it and how we might intervene effectively. Indeed, in recent years we have been able to identify a number of suicide-risk factors and there has been an increasing focus on these kinds of approaches.

However, Durkheim's discussion of suicide rates suggests that allowing the biological approach to dominate our thinking would be a mistake. His dismissal of nonsocial factors may have been ill advised, but *On Suicide's* demonstration of how rates vary between societies in connection with social variables such as integration (or the degree to which an individual is part of a given society) has now been supported by over a century of research. Durkheim's social causes of suicide are important. As Norwegian professor Heidi Hjelmeland* has pointed out, forgetting this "may have serious effects for our development as human beings."[3] Suicide is not only a symptom of certain mental health issues or purely the result of a genetic predisposition, so dealing with it as such is never going to be sufficient.

The text doesn't only challenge those who ignore the social nature of suicide, its authority also confronts those who believe the social nature of suicide should be studied in a different way. This has led to a number of attacks on the Durkheimian approach to suicide, in such works as Jack Douglas's* *The Social Meanings of Suicide* (1967) and Max Atkinson's* *Discovering Suicide: Studies in the Social Organization of Sudden Death* (1978).

The Continuing Debate

In recent years, a number of scholars, including sociology lecturer Ben Fincham,* have questioned the usefulness of Durkheim's distinction between the study of individual cases of suicide and the study of suicide rates. These scholars often argue that the focus on quantitative analysis of suicide rates, although not wrong, *has* limited sociology's contribution in this area. They have tried to show how the study of individual cases *can* inform a sociological understanding.

For example, Fincham tried to introduce a method of study that combines qualitative and quantitative approaches in order to "reinvigorate the sociology of suicide by moving out of the shadow of Durkheim."[4] For this group of scholars, Durkheim was wrong to argue that it is the situation and structure of the society in which people find themselves that wholly determines suicide. Fincham and others argue instead that people's actions and choices "work reciprocally with situations and structures, insofar as situations and structures are partly determined by choices made by individuals, and at the same time constrain and modify the choices available to them."[5]

Other scholars believe that Durkheim's account can be improved by incorporating some of the ideas of his intellectual rival, Gabriel Tarde.* For example, sociologists Seth Abrutyn* and Anna Mueller* argue that Durkheim's competitiveness with Tarde led him to reject the concept of imitation* as unsuitable for sociology. They believe that a great hole in Durkheim's theory—the question of which particular individual in a group will kill himself or herself—can be partly answered by using the social psychological concepts of imitation or contagion,* which, in Tarde's sociology, describes the spread of negative social actions or ideas. Abrutyn and Mueller argue that we should be careful "not to eliminate Durkheim as some critics have suggested … but rather to acknowledge the fact that social psychology must be considered a part of the study of suicide."[6]

It has also been argued that Durkheim's account of social integration was too simplistic. Based on evidence that suicide attempts by friends and family can trigger suicidal behavior in adolescents, Abrutyn and Mueller also suggest that social ties are not always supportive: in some circumstances they can actually *increase* the chance of suicidal behavior.[7] What matters then, is the structure and "content" (meaning the presence or absence of suicide behavior) of the social networks people belong to.[8] And by examining an individual's position within such a network, we can perhaps begin to understand why they choose suicide.

Even though more than a century has passed since Durkheim first published *On Suicide*, the debate over his account of voluntary death continues.

NOTES

1   Michael A. Overington, "A Rhetorical Appreciation of a Sociological Classic: Durkheim's 'Suicide,'" *Canadian Journal of Sociology* 6, no. 4 (1981): 448.

2   Overington, "A Rhetorical Appreciation," 457.

3   Heidi Hjelmeland, "Suicide Research and Prevention: The Importance of Culture in 'Biological Times,'" in *Suicide and Culture: Understanding the Context*, ed. Erminia Colucci and David Lester (Cambridge: Hogrefe Publishing, 2012), 5.

4   Ben Fincham, Susanne Langer, Jonathan Scourfield, and Michael Shiner, *Understanding Suicide: A Sociological Autopsy* (Basingstoke: Palgrave Macmillan, 2011), 169.

5   Fincham et al., *Understanding Suicide*, 170.

6   Seth Abrutyn and Anna Mueller, "Reconsidering Durkheim's Assessment of Tarde: Formalizing a Tardian Theory of Imitation, Contagion, and Suicide Suggestion," *Sociological Forum* 29, no. 3 (2014): 700.

7   Seth Abrutyn, Anna Mueller, and Cynthia Stockton, "Can Social Ties Be Harmful? Examining the Spread of Suicide in Early Adulthood," *Sociological Perspectives* 58, no. 2 (2015): 204–22.

8   Seth Abrutyn and Anna Mueller, "Are Suicidal Behaviors Contagious in Adolescence? Using Longitudinal Data to Examine Suicide Suggestion," *American Sociological Review* 79, no. 2 (2014): 211–27.

WHERE NEXT?

KEY POINTS

- It seems likely that sociologists* working on suicide will continue to use Émile Durkheim's 1897 work, *On Suicide*, to inspire their research.

- Durkheim's work shows how suicide is related to wider social issues, and while we cannot expect those same issues to apply today, it should still inspire sociologists to explore how large-scale social changes impact upon personal actions.

- *On Suicide* is a fundamentally important work because it so vividly demonstrates the power of the sociological imagination: it maneuvers skillfully around research obstacles to teach us something novel about the world we live in.

Potential

Émile Durkheim's *On Suicide* is one of the great classics of sociology. Its influence reaches well beyond the field of suicide studies. Durkheim explored the rare phenomenon of suicide partly because he felt it could tell us something about more everyday behavior. For Durkheim, suicide is the ultimate way in which individuals cut themselves off from society. By trying to understand how human bonds could become fragile enough to allow this, Durkheim also believed he might discover what makes them strong. So *On Suicide* is not just about why people kill themselves. Like his other great works, it is also about how society is held together. As this is a central concern in sociology, the concepts developed in *On Suicide* have become applicable to the research of sociologists working in a number of different fields.

> **"** [Durkheim's] fundamental assertion remains: even the seemingly personal act of suicide demands a sociological explanation. **"**
>
> Anthony Giddens, *Sociology*

Unfortunately, the text's wider influence has not translated into increased sociological research on suicide itself. Most discussions circle around an analysis of the text itself—a situation that prompted the respected sociologist Jack Gibbs* to suggest that "sociologists should rightly proclaim Durkheim to have been a genius, and then get on with it."[1] This does not mean we have to abandon Durkheim's model, not least because that model has vast potential to be extended. Rather, we need to appreciate the potential for Durkheim's work to contribute to the conversations about suicide occurring *outside* sociology and, likewise, the potential for these conversations to enhance Durkheim's own framework. This project is beginning to take hold. Scholars such as Seth Abrutyn* and Anna Mueller,* for example, have looked at how to integrate advances from psychology*, social psychology,* and psychiatry* into Durkheim's basic model.[2]

Future Directions

Abrutyn and Mueller's work shows that we are still only beginning to understand just how complex many of the general relationships Durkheim identified really are. With social conditions changing all the time, these will need to be continually reassessed. Moreover, as we learn more about which individuals are in particular danger through, for instance, genetic and biochemical approaches, we need to understand how this relates to the regularities and patterns of suicide rates. Durkheim's framework will be of help here, but we must continue to make improvements.

One way to do this, in addition to putting advances from other disciplines into Durkheim's model, is to bring *On Suicide* into greater harmony with contemporary social theory. Sociology professor Bernice Pescosolido* and her colleagues, for example, have had success interpreting Durkheim's framework through social network theory.*[3] Social network theory is an approach to social analysis that focuses on mapping the relationships between people. It is also known as network analysis.

The networks mapped by these studies appear to have much in common with Durkheim's groups, and offer a way to reach greater specific understanding. Another way to extend Durkheim's theory, encouraged in sociologist Matt Wray's* 2011 coauthored article on suicide research,[4] is to look at how qualitative* methods allow us to investigate whether and how the meaning of suicide in each of Durkheim's four conditions (egoism,* altruism,* anomie,* and fatalism*) compares from one to another. Does suicide mean the same thing to people when social integration is low as it does when it is high? Are suicides interpreted differently in situations of anomie from how they are in situations of egoism? These are just some of the questions thrown up by Durkheim's text as we seek to advance our overall understanding of suicide.

Sociology has fallen quiet on the subject of suicide over the last few decades.[5] But as Durkheim's text shows, the sociological perspective can contribute a great deal toward understanding the subject; tomorrow's sociologists need to make sure that lesson is not forgotten.

Summary

Durkheim's *On Suicide* reminds us that the question "Why did that person kill him/herself?" is not the only important one to ask about suicide. We should also ask why more people kill themselves in some groups than in other groups. The answer is not always obvious, but in finding it, we might learn how to reduce the number of suicides in the future.

Durkheim was hardly the first to note the patterned nature of suicide rates, and his description of them was not the primary reason for *On Suicide's* impact. His ability to bring a sophisticated sociological approach to their analysis was key. Today we know this had flaws. There were problems with his statistical methods as well as with his raw data. So it is perhaps all the more impressive that the framework Durkheim managed to construct from his material still to this day defines the shape and direction of most sociological research on suicide. And it does not look as if we are going to stop using it any time soon; Durkheim's general approach is still productive, useful, and insightful.

The famous French novelist and philosopher Albert Camus* once claimed that there is only one philosophical question that really genuinely matters, and that is whether life is worth living. Writing before Camus, Durkheim saw this from a sociological viewpoint, and looked at suicide in the hope that it might provide some answers. But as a sociologist, he recognized that we are never in isolation when we ask this question. We are embedded within societies, and the way we answer it is affected by the condition of these societies. There is no single correct response. We can only ask, as Durkheim did, "Under what social conditions are people likely to decide society isn't worth being in?" And if we can understand these conditions, well, then we will have found out something truly valuable about our own existence.

NOTES

1   Jack Gibbs, as quoted in Ben Fincham, Susanne Langer, Jonathan Scourfield, and Michael Shiner, *Understanding Suicide: A Sociological Autopsy* (Basingstoke: Palgrave Macmillan, 2011), 30.

2   Seth Abrutyn and Anna Mueller, "The Socioemotional Foundations of Suicide: a Microsociological View of Durkheim's Suicide," *Sociological Theory* 32, no. 4 (2014): 327–51.

3   Bernice Pescosolido and Sharon Georgianna, "Durkheim, Suicide, and Religion: Toward a Network Theory of Suicide," *American Sociological Review* 54 (1989): 33–48; Bernice Pescosolido, "Of Pride and Prejudice: The Role of Sociology and Social Networks in Integrating the Health Sciences," *Journal of Health and Social Behavior* 47 (2006): 189–208.

4   Matt Wray, Cynthia Colen, and Bernice Pescosolido, "The Sociology of Suicide," *Annual Review of Sociology* 37 (2011): 505–28.

5   Steven Stack and Barbara Bowman, *Suicide Movies: Social Patterns 1900–2009* (Cambridge, MA: Hogrefe, 2012).

GLOSSARY

GLOSSARY OF TERMS

Altruism: in Durkheimian terminology, an undesirably high level of social integration.

Anomie: in Durkheimian terminology, a lack of social regulation.

Capitalism: an economic system based on competition and the pursuit of profit.

Roman Catholic: a Christian who accepts the authority of the Pope (the Bishop of Rome).

Contagion: usually the transfer of disease from one individual to another. In Gabriel Tarde's sociology, however, it describes the spread of negative social actions or ideas.

Criminology: the scientific study of crime and criminals.

Cultural sociology: this school of sociology emphasizes the cultural character of all social phenomena. Cultural sociologists often use concepts like "collective emotion" and "collective idea" in their explanations. The term was popularized by Jeffrey Alexander.

Deconstructivism: a form of critical analysis developed by the French philosopher Jacques Derrida (1930–2004) that draws attention to the instability of meaning.

École Normale Supérieure: one of the higher education establishments in France that remains outside the public university system. Thirteen Nobel Prize laureates were educated at this school.

Egoism: in Durkheimian terminology, an undesirably low level of social integration.

Empirical sociology: a branch of sociology, popular today, that emphasizes the use of statistical techniques to analyze the results of tests or observations.

Empiricism/empirical approach: the idea that all knowledge should be gained by experience—that is, by using experiments and observation to gather facts.

Fatalism: in Durkheimian terminology, an undesirably high level of social regulation.

Functionalism: the sociological perspective that analyses how social institutions contribute to the working of society as a whole.

Genetics: the study of inherited characteristics.

Heredity: the passing of characteristics, mental or physical, from generation to generation.

Imitation: when an individual copies the behavior of another individual. Gabriel Tarde made this concept the center of his sociology.

Industrialization: the shift toward increasingly using machines to complete tasks, usually in the work environment.

Innovation: the process of making an object, practice or idea that is believed to be new. The result of this process can also be called an innovation.

Interpretivism: in sociology, this refers to a mode of research that tries to interpret the meaning of human behavior in context rather than look for generalizations.

Interwar period (1919–39): the years between the end of World War I and the start of World War II.

Moral statisticians: a group of nineteenth-century scholars who believed that statistical information can tell us about the moral status of society.

Orthodox Judaism: the traditional practices and beliefs of Judaism.

Positivism: a philosophy that regards only scientifically verifiable facts and laws as authoritative knowledge.

Post-communism: the period following the communist era. Communism is an ideology and movement associated with the ideas of Karl Marx (1818–83) that seeks common ownership of the means of production.

Postmodernism: a school of thought characterized by its rejection of the values and assumptions of (Western) modernity. In particular, postmodern philosophy has been skeptical about the power of reason.

Protestantism: a form of Christianity that rejects the authority of the Pope and emphasizes the importance of reading the Bible.

Psychiatry: the study of mental illness.

Psychology: the study of the mind and its functions, and how it affects behavior.

Qualitative research: research that studies aspects of the world that cannot be measured in numbers.

Quantitative research: research using statistical or mathematical techniques.

Rabbi: a teacher and expert interpreter of Jewish law.

Ritual: a defined set of actions performed regularly. Durkheim argued that rituals play an important role in reinforcing the link between individuals and their community.

Sacred: Durkheim defined sacred objects as things that are prohibited and set apart.

Social fact: in Durkheim's sociology this is something that exists externally to individuals. Social facts constrain our behavior and drive us to act in certain ways. These constraints include social norms and social structures.

Social integration: the degree to which members of society are bound together.

Social network theory: an approach to social analysis that focuses on mapping the relationships between people. It is also known as network analysis.

Social psychology: the area of psychology that investigates social interactions, where those social interactions come from, and their effects on the individual.

Social regulation: the control that social values and norms have over individuals.

Social solidarity: the degree to which individuals are connected to social groups.

Social suicide rate: The number of suicides in a set place over a set period of time.

Sociology: the study of our social world's structure and development.

Sorbonne: this refers generally to the University of Paris. However, the term also refers to the historical building in Paris housing (in whole or part) a number of universities and research institutions.

Structuralism: a school of thought that suggests that elements of human culture can only be understood in terms of their relations with other elements. These networks of relations constitute the "structure" of society.

Third Republic: the government of France from 1879 to 1940.

World War I (1914–18): this was a major conflict involving all of the main European powers (primarily Germany, France, and Great Britain) and a number of other world powers, including the United States and Japan.

World War II (1939–45): a global conflict fought between the Axis Powers (Germany, Italy, and Japan) and the victorious Allied Powers (the United Kingdom and its colonies, the Soviet Union, and the United States).

Yeshiva: a Jewish institution where the religious texts of Judaism are studied.

PEOPLE MENTIONED IN THE TEXT

Seth Abrutyn is assistant professor of sociology at the University of Memphis and specializes in social theory. His most important work is *Revisiting Institutionalism in Sociology: Putting the "Institution" Back in Institutional Analysis* (2013).

Jeffery C. Alexander (b. 1947) has been a key figure both in the revival of Talcott Parsons's functionalist sociology, and in cultural sociology. Important works include *The Meanings of Social Life* (2003) and *Performance and Power* (2011).

Max Atkinson is a former fellow of Wolfson College, Oxford. Since the mid-1980s he has been using the results of research into public speaking to coach speakers, run courses, and write books about communicating effectively.

Henri-Louis Bergson (1859–1941) was an influential French philosopher who, in contrast to Durkheim, emphasized the importance of intuition and immediate experience for understanding the world around us.

Émile Boutroux (1845–1921) was an important thinker whose work can be included in the school of philosophy termed "French spiritualism." Significant texts include *The Contingency of the Laws of Nature* (1874) and *Historical Studies in Philosophy* (1897).

Albert Camus (1913–60) was a French novelist, journalist and philosopher. He was awarded the Nobel Prize for Literature in 1957.

Auguste Comte (1798–1857) was the founder of positivism (a philosophy that regards only scientifically verifiable facts and laws as authoritative knowledge). He is widely regarded as the first modern philosopher of science.

Jack Douglas is an emeritus professor of sociology at the University of California, San Diego. He is best known for his book *The Social Meanings of Suicide* (1967).

Alfred Espinas (1844–1922) was a French scholar who studied under both Auguste Comte and Herbert Spencer.

Jean-Étienne Esquirol (1772–1840) was a French psychiatrist. His most important work was *Mental Maladies: A Treatise on Insanity* (1838).

Ben Fincham is a senior lecturer in sociology at Sussex University. His research interests include the sociology of cycling, suicide, and happiness.

Jack Gibbs is the Centennial Professor and Chair of Sociology and Anthropology Emeritus at Vanderbilt University. His more than 170 publications include *Sociological Theory Construction* (1972), *Crime, Punishment, and Deterrence* (1975), and *Norms, Deviance, and Social Control: Conceptual Matters* (1981).

Anthony Giddens (b. 1938) is a British sociologist who has had a strong influence on both domestic and international politics. Key texts include *The Constitution of Society* (1984) and *The Third Way: The Renewal of Social Democracy* (1998).

Maurice Halbwachs (1877–1945) was a French sociologist and philosopher. He is best known for his work on the concept of collective memory and his book *Les causes du suicide* (1930).

Peter Hamilton (b.1948) is a British sociologist. He has published widely on the sociology of photography and classic social theory.

Heidi Hjelmeland (b. 1960) is a professor in the department of social work and health science at the Norwegian University of Science and Technology. Suicide is her primary area of research and she has published extensively on this subject.

Victor Hommay (d. 1886) was one of Durkheim's closest friends at school. He is believed to have taken his own life.

Barclay DeLay Johnson gained his PhD in sociology from the University of California at Berkley in 1960. His most famous work is *Emile Durkheim and the Theory of Social Integration* (1964).

Xavier Léon (1868–1935) was a French philosopher best known for his work on Johann Fichte. His works include *Fichte et son temps* (1922).

Claude Lévi-Strauss (1908–2009) was an anthropologist who developed a school of thought known as structuralism. His most important works include *Structural Anthropology* (1958) and *The Savage Mind* (1962).

Steven Lukes (b. 1941) is a professor of politics and sociology at New York University. His best-known book is *Power: A Radical View* (first published in 1974), in which he sets out a three-dimensional view of power.

Marcel Mauss (1872–1950) was a sociologist and anthropologist whose most famous text is *The Gift: Forms and Functions of Exchange in Archaic Societies* (1925). He was also Émile Durkheim's nephew.

Stjepan G. Meštrović (b. 1955) is a sociologist known for his work on war crimes. Texts include *Durkheim and Postmodern Culture* (1992) and *The Trials of Abu Ghraib: An Expert Witness Account of Shame and Honor* (2007).

Anna S. Mueller is assistant professor of sociology at the University of Memphis. Her fields of interest include health and wellbeing in adolescents.

Michael Overington was a professor of sociology at St Mary's University, Halifax. His publications include the coauthored book *Organizations as Theatre: A Social Psychology of Dramatic Appearances* (1987).

Talcott Parsons (1902–79) was an American sociologist whose most famous work, *The Structure of Social Action* (1937), tried to synthesize the thought of important theorists such as Durkheim, Weber, and Pareto. The outcome was Parsons' "social action theory."

Bernice A. Pescosolido is a distinguished professor of sociology at Indiana University. She has written numerous articles and book chapters on the sociology of mental health and illness and has also edited a number of books, including *The SAGE Handbook of Mental Health and Illness* (2010).

Adolphe Quetelet (1796–1874) was one of the first scholars to use statistics to study the social world. One of his many notable achievements was the invention of the body mass index (BMI).

Ferdinand de Saussure (1857–1913) was a Swiss linguist whose most important work, *Course in General Linguistics* (1916), was published posthumously by former students. The work's key argument is that we understand the meaning of a sentence or word because we know how it relates to other possible meanings.

Eugen Schoenfeld (b. 1925) is a Holocaust survivor and emeritus professor and chair of the Georgia State University Sociology Department. Published works include his autobiography, *My Reconstructed Life* (2005).

Herbert Spencer (1820–1903) was an English thinker who made contributions to philosophy, sociology, biology, and other fields. He is perhaps most famous for coining the term "survival of the fittest."

Gabriel Tarde (1843–1904) was a statistician, magistrate, criminologist, and sociologist. Important works include *Les lois de l'imitation* (1890; translated as *The Laws of Imitation*).

Ferdinand Tönnies (1855–1936) was an early German sociologist whose classic work *Community and Society* (1887) drew a distinction between groups based on contractual ties and those based on "organic" feelings of togetherness.

Max Weber (1864–1920) is widely considered one of the three founders of sociology. His most famous work is *The Protestant Ethic and the Spirit of Capitalism* (1905).

Matt Wray is associate professor of sociology at Temple University. In addition to the sociology of suicide, his research interests include race and ethnicity, particularly the stigmatization of poor rural white communities in America.

Wu Fei (b. 1973) is a professor of philosophy and religious studies at Peking University. His research interests include suicide in Christianity and Chinese culture.

WORKS CITED

WORKS CITED

Abrutyn, Seth, and Anna Mueller. "Reconsidering Durkheim's Assessment of Tarde: Formalizing a Tardian Theory of Imitation, Contagion, and Suicide Suggestion." *Sociological Forum* 29, no. 3 (2014): 698–719.

"The Socioemotional Foundations of Suicide: a Microsociological View of Durkheim's Suicide." *Sociological Theory* 32, no. 4 (2014): 327–51.

"Are Suicidal Behaviors Contagious in Adolescence? Using Longitudinal Data to Examine Suicide Suggestion." *American Sociological Review* 79, no. 2 (2014): 211–27.

Abrutyn, Seth, Anna Mueller, and Cynthia Stockton. "Can Social Ties Be Harmful? Examining the Spread of Suicide in Early Adulthood." *Sociological Perspectives* 58, no. 2 (2015): 204–22.

Alexander, Jeffrey C. "The Inner Development of Durkheim's Sociological Theory: From Early Writings to Maturity." In *The Cambridge Companion to Durkheim*, edited by Jeffrey C. Alexander and Phillip Smith, 136–59. Cambridge: Cambridge University Press, 2005.

Atkinson, J. Maxwell. *Discovering Suicide: Studies in the Social Organization of Sudden Death.* Pittsburgh: University of Pittsburgh Press, 1978.

Collins, Randall. "The Durkheimian Movement in France and in World Sociology." In *The Cambridge Companion to Durkheim*, edited by Jeffrey C. Alexander and Phillip Smith, 101–35. Cambridge: Cambridge University Press, 2005.

Douglas, Jack. *The Social Meanings of Suicide.* Princeton, NJ: Princeton University Press, 1967.

Durkheim, Émile. *The Division of Labour in Society.* Translated by W. D. Halls. Basingstoke: Palgrave Macmillan, 2013.

The Elementary Forms of Religious Life. Translated by C. Cosman. Oxford: Oxford University Press, 2008.

On Suicide. Translated by Robin Buss. London: Penguin Books, 2006.

The Rules of Sociological Method: and Selected Texts on Sociology and Its Method. Translated by W. D. Halls. London: Macmillan, 1982.

Suicide. Translated by J. A. Spaulding and G. Simpson. London: Routledge, 2002.

Esquirol, Jean Etienne Dominique. *Mental Maladies: a Treatise on Insanity*. Translated by E. K. Hunt. Published under the auspices of the Library of the New York Academy of Medicine by Hafner, 1965.

Fincham, Ben, Susanne Langer, Jonathan Scourfield, and Michael Shiner. *Understanding Suicide: A Sociological Autopsy.* Basingstoke: Palgrave Macmillan, 2011.

Giddens, Anthony. *Capitalism and Modern Social Theory: An Analysis of the Writings of Marx, Durkheim and Max Weber.* London: Cambridge University Press, 1971.

Giddens, Anthony. *Durkheim.* London: Fontana Press, 1978.

Sociology, 5th ed. Cambridge: Polity Press, 2006.

"The Suicide Problem in French Sociology." *British Journal of Sociology* 16, no. 1 (1965): 3–18.

Goldney, Robert D. and Johan A. Schioldann. "Evolution of the Concept of Altruistic Suicide in Pre-Durkheim Suicidology." *Archives of Suicide Research* 8, no. 1 (2004): 23–7.

Hamilton, Peter. "Introductory Essay: Emile Durkheim." In *Emile Durkheim: Critical Assessments*, edited by Peter Hamilton, 3–8. London: Routledge, 1995.

Hjelmeland, Heidi. "Suicide Research and Prevention: The Importance of Culture in 'Biological Times.'" In *Suicide and Culture: Understanding the Context*, edited by Erminia Colucci and David Lester, 3–24. Cambridge: Hogrefe Publishing, 2012.

Johnson, Barclay D. "Durkheim's One Cause of Suicide." *American Sociological Review* 30, no. 6 (1965): 865–86.

Lukes, Steven. *Émile Durkheim: His Life and Work.* Harmondsworth: Penguin, 1975.

Overington, Michael A. "A Rhetorical Appreciation of a Sociological Classic: Durkheim's 'Suicide.'" *Canadian Journal of Sociology* 6, no. 4 (1981): 447–61.

Pescosolido, Bernice. "Of Pride and Prejudice: The Role of Sociology and Social Networks in Integrating the Health Sciences." *Journal of Health and Social Behavior* 47 (2006): 189–208.

Pescosolido, Bernice, and Sharon Georgianna. "Durkheim, Suicide, and Religion: Toward a Network Theory of Suicide." *American Sociological Review* 54 (1989): 33–48.

Pope, Whitney. *Durkheim's Suicide: A Classic Analyzed.* Chicago: University of Chicago Press, 1976.

Schoenfeld, Eugen, and Stjepan G. Meštrović. "Durkheim's Concept of Justice and its Relationship to Social Solidarity." *Sociological Analysis* 50, no. 2 (1989): 111–27.

Smith, Phillip, and Jeffrey C. Alexander. "Introduction: The New Durkheim." In *The Cambridge Companion to Durkheim*, edited by Jeffrey C. Alexander and Phillip Smith, 1–40. Cambridge: Cambridge University Press, 2005.

Stack, Steven, and Barbara Bowman. *Suicide Movies: Social Patterns 1900–2009*. Cambridge, MA: Hogrefe, 2012.

Vargas, E. V., B. Latour, B. Karsenti, F. Aït-Touati, and L. Salmon. "The Debate between Tarde and Durkheim." *Environment and Planning D: Society and Space* 26, no. 5 (2008): 761–77.

Wray, Matt, Cynthia Colen, and Bernice Pescosolido. "The Sociology of Suicide." *Annual Review of Sociology* 37 (2011): 505–28.

Wu Fei. *Suicide and Justice: A Chinese Perspective.* London and New York: Routledge, 2010.

THE MACAT LIBRARY
BY DISCIPLINE

The Macat Library By Discipline

AFRICANA STUDIES

Chinua Achebe's *An Image of Africa: Racism in Conrad's Heart of Darkness*
W. E. B. Du Bois's *The Souls of Black Folk*
Zora Neale Huston's *Characteristics of Negro Expression*
Martin Luther King Jr's *Why We Can't Wait*
Toni Morrison's *Playing in the Dark: Whiteness in the American Literary Imagination*

ANTHROPOLOGY

Arjun Appadurai's *Modernity at Large: Cultural Dimensions of Globalisation*
Philippe Ariès's *Centuries of Childhood*
Franz Boas's *Race, Language and Culture*
Kim Chan & Renée Mauborgne's *Blue Ocean Strategy*
Jared Diamond's *Guns, Germs & Steel: the Fate of Human Societies*
Jared Diamond's *Collapse: How Societies Choose to Fail or Survive*
E. E. Evans-Pritchard's *Witchcraft, Oracles and Magic Among the Azande*
James Ferguson's *The Anti-Politics Machine*
Clifford Geertz's *The Interpretation of Cultures*
David Graeber's *Debt: the First 5000 Years*
Karen Ho's *Liquidated: An Ethnography of Wall Street*
Geert Hofstede's *Culture's Consequences: Comparing Values, Behaviors, Institutes and Organizations across Nations*
Claude Lévi-Strauss's *Structural Anthropology*
Jay Macleod's *Ain't No Makin' It: Aspirations and Attainment in a Low-Income Neighborhood*
Saba Mahmood's *The Politics of Piety: The Islamic Revival and the Feminist Subject*
Marcel Mauss's *The Gift*

BUSINESS

Jean Lave & Etienne Wenger's *Situated Learning*
Theodore Levitt's *Marketing Myopia*
Burton G. Malkiel's *A Random Walk Down Wall Street*
Douglas McGregor's *The Human Side of Enterprise*
Michael Porter's *Competitive Strategy: Creating and Sustaining Superior Performance*
John Kotter's *Leading Change*
C. K. Prahalad & Gary Hamel's *The Core Competence of the Corporation*

CRIMINOLOGY

Michelle Alexander's *The New Jim Crow: Mass Incarceration in the Age of Colorblindness*
Michael R. Gottfredson & Travis Hirschi's *A General Theory of Crime*
Richard Herrnstein & Charles A. Murray's *The Bell Curve: Intelligence and Class Structure in American Life*
Elizabeth Loftus's *Eyewitness Testimony*
Jay Macleod's *Ain't No Makin' It: Aspirations and Attainment in a Low-Income Neighborhood*
Philip Zimbardo's *The Lucifer Effect*

ECONOMICS

Janet Abu-Lughod's *Before European Hegemony*
Ha-Joon Chang's *Kicking Away the Ladder*
David Brion Davis's *The Problem of Slavery in the Age of Revolution*
Milton Friedman's *The Role of Monetary Policy*
Milton Friedman's *Capitalism and Freedom*
David Graeber's *Debt: the First 5000 Years*
Friedrich Hayek's *The Road to Serfdom*
Karen Ho's *Liquidated: An Ethnography of Wall Street*

John Maynard Keynes's *The General Theory of Employment, Interest and Money*
Charles P. Kindleberger's *Manias, Panics and Crashes*
Robert Lucas's *Why Doesn't Capital Flow from Rich to Poor Countries?*
Burton G. Malkiel's *A Random Walk Down Wall Street*
Thomas Robert Malthus's *An Essay on the Principle of Population*
Karl Marx's *Capital*
Thomas Piketty's *Capital in the Twenty-First Century*
Amartya Sen's *Development as Freedom*
Adam Smith's *The Wealth of Nations*
Nassim Nicholas Taleb's *The Black Swan: The Impact of the Highly Improbable*
Amos Tversky's & Daniel Kahneman's *Judgment under Uncertainty: Heuristics and Biases*
Mahbub Ul Haq's *Reflections on Human Development*
Max Weber's *The Protestant Ethic and the Spirit of Capitalism*

FEMINISM AND GENDER STUDIES

Judith Butler's *Gender Trouble*
Simone De Beauvoir's *The Second Sex*
Michel Foucault's *History of Sexuality*
Betty Friedan's *The Feminine Mystique*
Saba Mahmood's *The Politics of Piety: The Islamic Revival and the Feminist Subject*
Joan Wallach Scott's *Gender and the Politics of History*
Mary Wollstonecraft's *A Vindication of the Rights of Woman*
Virginia Woolf's *A Room of One's Own*

GEOGRAPHY

The Brundtland Report's *Our Common Future*
Rachel Carson's *Silent Spring*
Charles Darwin's *On the Origin of Species*
James Ferguson's *The Anti-Politics Machine*
Jane Jacobs's *The Death and Life of Great American Cities*
James Lovelock's *Gaia: A New Look at Life on Earth*
Amartya Sen's *Development as Freedom*
Mathis Wackernagel & William Rees's *Our Ecological Footprint*

HISTORY

Janet Abu-Lughod's *Before European Hegemony*
Benedict Anderson's *Imagined Communities*
Bernard Bailyn's *The Ideological Origins of the American Revolution*
Hanna Batatu's *The Old Social Classes And The Revolutionary Movements Of Iraq*
Christopher Browning's *Ordinary Men: Reserve Police Batallion 101 and the Final Solution in Poland*
Edmund Burke's *Reflections on the Revolution in France*
William Cronon's *Nature's Metropolis: Chicago And The Great West*
Alfred W. Crosby's *The Columbian Exchange*
Hamid Dabashi's *Iran: A People Interrupted*
David Brion Davis's *The Problem of Slavery in the Age of Revolution*
Nathalie Zemon Davis's *The Return of Martin Guerre*
Jared Diamond's *Guns, Germs & Steel: the Fate of Human Societies*
Frank Dikotter's *Mao's Great Famine*
John W Dower's *War Without Mercy: Race And Power In The Pacific War*
W. E. B. Du Bois's *The Souls of Black Folk*
Richard J. Evans's *In Defence of History*
Lucien Febvre's *The Problem of Unbelief in the 16th Century*
Sheila Fitzpatrick's *Everyday Stalinism*

The Macat Library By Discipline

Eric Foner's *Reconstruction: America's Unfinished Revolution, 1863-1877*
Michel Foucault's *Discipline and Punish*
Michel Foucault's *History of Sexuality*
Francis Fukuyama's *The End of History and the Last Man*
John Lewis Gaddis's *We Now Know: Rethinking Cold War History*
Ernest Gellner's *Nations and Nationalism*
Eugene Genovese's *Roll, Jordan, Roll: The World the Slaves Made*
Carlo Ginzburg's *The Night Battles*
Daniel Goldhagen's *Hitler's Willing Executioners*
Jack Goldstone's *Revolution and Rebellion in the Early Modern World*
Antonio Gramsci's *The Prison Notebooks*
Alexander Hamilton, John Jay & James Madison's *The Federalist Papers*
Christopher Hill's *The World Turned Upside Down*
Carole Hillenbrand's *The Crusades: Islamic Perspectives*
Thomas Hobbes's *Leviathan*
Eric Hobsbawm's *The Age Of Revolution*
John A. Hobson's *Imperialism: A Study*
Albert Hourani's *History of the Arab Peoples*
Samuel P. Huntington's *The Clash of Civilizations and the Remaking of World Order*
C. L. R. James's *The Black Jacobins*
Tony Judt's *Postwar: A History of Europe Since 1945*
Ernst Kantorowicz's *The King's Two Bodies: A Study in Medieval Political Theology*
Paul Kennedy's *The Rise and Fall of the Great Powers*
Ian Kershaw's *The "Hitler Myth": Image and Reality in the Third Reich*
John Maynard Keynes's *The General Theory of Employment, Interest and Money*
Charles P. Kindleberger's *Manias, Panics and Crashes*
Martin Luther King Jr's *Why We Can't Wait*
Henry Kissinger's *World Order: Reflections on the Character of Nations and the Course of History*
Thomas Kuhn's *The Structure of Scientific Revolutions*
Georges Lefebvre's *The Coming of the French Revolution*
John Locke's *Two Treatises of Government*
Niccolò Machiavelli's *The Prince*
Thomas Robert Malthus's *An Essay on the Principle of Population*
Mahmood Mamdani's *Citizen and Subject: Contemporary Africa And The Legacy Of Late Colonialism*
Karl Marx's *Capital*
Stanley Milgram's *Obedience to Authority*
John Stuart Mill's *On Liberty*
Thomas Paine's *Common Sense*
Thomas Paine's *Rights of Man*
Geoffrey Parker's *Global Crisis: War, Climate Change and Catastrophe in the Seventeenth Century*
Jonathan Riley-Smith's *The First Crusade and the Idea of Crusading*
Jean-Jacques Rousseau's *The Social Contract*
Joan Wallach Scott's *Gender and the Politics of History*
Theda Skocpol's *States and Social Revolutions*
Adam Smith's *The Wealth of Nations*
Timothy Snyder's *Bloodlands: Europe Between Hitler and Stalin*
Sun Tzu's *The Art of War*
Keith Thomas's *Religion and the Decline of Magic*
Thucydides's *The History of the Peloponnesian War*
Frederick Jackson Turner's *The Significance of the Frontier in American History*
Odd Arne Westad's *The Global Cold War: Third World Interventions And The Making Of Our Times*

LITERATURE

Chinua Achebe's *An Image of Africa: Racism in Conrad's Heart of Darkness*
Roland Barthes's *Mythologies*
Homi K. Bhabha's *The Location of Culture*
Judith Butler's *Gender Trouble*
Simone De Beauvoir's *The Second Sex*
Ferdinand De Saussure's *Course in General Linguistics*
T. S. Eliot's *The Sacred Wood: Essays on Poetry and Criticism*
Zora Neale Huston's *Characteristics of Negro Expression*
Toni Morrison's *Playing in the Dark: Whiteness in the American Literary Imagination*
Edward Said's *Orientalism*
Gayatri Chakravorty Spivak's *Can the Subaltern Speak?*
Mary Wollstonecraft's *A Vindication of the Rights of Women*
Virginia Woolf's *A Room of One's Own*

PHILOSOPHY

Elizabeth Anscombe's *Modern Moral Philosophy*
Hannah Arendt's *The Human Condition*
Aristotle's *Metaphysics*
Aristotle's *Nicomachean Ethics*
Edmund Gettier's *Is Justified True Belief Knowledge?*
Georg Wilhelm Friedrich Hegel's *Phenomenology of Spirit*
David Hume's *Dialogues Concerning Natural Religion*
David Hume's *The Enquiry for Human Understanding*
Immanuel Kant's *Religion within the Boundaries of Mere Reason*
Immanuel Kant's *Critique of Pure Reason*
Søren Kierkegaard's *The Sickness Unto Death*
Søren Kierkegaard's *Fear and Trembling*
C. S. Lewis's *The Abolition of Man*
Alasdair MacIntyre's *After Virtue*
Marcus Aurelius's *Meditations*
Friedrich Nietzsche's *On the Genealogy of Morality*
Friedrich Nietzsche's *Beyond Good and Evil*
Plato's *Republic*
Plato's *Symposium*
Jean-Jacques Rousseau's *The Social Contract*
Gilbert Ryle's *The Concept of Mind*
Baruch Spinoza's *Ethics*
Sun Tzu's *The Art of War*
Ludwig Wittgenstein's *Philosophical Investigations*

POLITICS

Benedict Anderson's *Imagined Communities*
Aristotle's *Politics*
Bernard Bailyn's *The Ideological Origins of the American Revolution*
Edmund Burke's *Reflections on the Revolution in France*
John C. Calhoun's *A Disquisition on Government*
Ha-Joon Chang's *Kicking Away the Ladder*
Hamid Dabashi's *Iran: A People Interrupted*
Hamid Dabashi's *Theology of Discontent: The Ideological Foundation of the Islamic Revolution in Iran*
Robert Dahl's *Democracy and its Critics*
Robert Dahl's *Who Governs?*
David Brion Davis's *The Problem of Slavery in the Age of Revolution*

The Macat Library By Discipline

Alexis De Tocqueville's *Democracy in America*
James Ferguson's *The Anti-Politics Machine*
Frank Dikotter's *Mao's Great Famine*
Sheila Fitzpatrick's *Everyday Stalinism*
Eric Foner's *Reconstruction: America's Unfinished Revolution, 1863-1877*
Milton Friedman's *Capitalism and Freedom*
Francis Fukuyama's *The End of History and the Last Man*
John Lewis Gaddis's *We Now Know: Rethinking Cold War History*
Ernest Gellner's *Nations and Nationalism*
David Graeber's *Debt: the First 5000 Years*
Antonio Gramsci's *The Prison Notebooks*
Alexander Hamilton, John Jay & James Madison's *The Federalist Papers*
Friedrich Hayek's *The Road to Serfdom*
Christopher Hill's *The World Turned Upside Down*
Thomas Hobbes's *Leviathan*
John A. Hobson's *Imperialism: A Study*
Samuel P. Huntington's *The Clash of Civilizations and the Remaking of World Order*
Tony Judt's *Postwar: A History of Europe Since 1945*
David C. Kang's *China Rising: Peace, Power and Order in East Asia*
Paul Kennedy's *The Rise and Fall of Great Powers*
Robert Keohane's *After Hegemony*
Martin Luther King Jr.'s *Why We Can't Wait*
Henry Kissinger's *World Order: Reflections on the Character of Nations and the Course of History*
John Locke's *Two Treatises of Government*
Niccolò Machiavelli's *The Prince*
Thomas Robert Malthus's *An Essay on the Principle of Population*
Mahmood Mamdani's *Citizen and Subject: Contemporary Africa And The Legacy Of Late Colonialism*
Karl Marx's *Capital*
John Stuart Mill's *On Liberty*
John Stuart Mill's *Utilitarianism*
Hans Morgenthau's *Politics Among Nations*
Thomas Paine's *Common Sense*
Thomas Paine's *Rights of Man*
Thomas Piketty's *Capital in the Twenty-First Century*
Robert D. Putman's *Bowling Alone*
John Rawls's *Theory of Justice*
Jean-Jacques Rousseau's *The Social Contract*
Theda Skocpol's *States and Social Revolutions*
Adam Smith's *The Wealth of Nations*
Sun Tzu's *The Art of War*
Henry David Thoreau's *Civil Disobedience*
Thucydides's *The History of the Peloponnesian War*
Kenneth Waltz's *Theory of International Politics*
Max Weber's *Politics as a Vocation*
Odd Arne Westad's *The Global Cold War: Third World Interventions And The Making Of Our Times*

POSTCOLONIAL STUDIES

Roland Barthes's *Mythologies*
Frantz Fanon's *Black Skin, White Masks*
Homi K. Bhabha's *The Location of Culture*
Gustavo Gutiérrez's *A Theology of Liberation*
Edward Said's *Orientalism*
Gayatri Chakravorty Spivak's *Can the Subaltern Speak?*

PSYCHOLOGY

Gordon Allport's *The Nature of Prejudice*
Alan Baddeley & Graham Hitch's *Aggression: A Social Learning Analysis*
Albert Bandura's *Aggression: A Social Learning Analysis*
Leon Festinger's *A Theory of Cognitive Dissonance*
Sigmund Freud's *The Interpretation of Dreams*
Betty Friedan's *The Feminine Mystique*
Michael R. Gottfredson & Travis Hirschi's *A General Theory of Crime*
Eric Hoffer's *The True Believer: Thoughts on the Nature of Mass Movements*
William James's *Principles of Psychology*
Elizabeth Loftus's *Eyewitness Testimony*
A. H. Maslow's *A Theory of Human Motivation*
Stanley Milgram's *Obedience to Authority*
Steven Pinker's *The Better Angels of Our Nature*
Oliver Sacks's *The Man Who Mistook His Wife For a Hat*
Richard Thaler & Cass Sunstein's *Nudge: Improving Decisions About Health, Wealth and Happiness*
Amos Tversky's *Judgment under Uncertainty: Heuristics and Biases*
Philip Zimbardo's *The Lucifer Effect*

SCIENCE

Rachel Carson's *Silent Spring*
William Cronon's *Nature's Metropolis: Chicago And The Great West*
Alfred W. Crosby's *The Columbian Exchange*
Charles Darwin's *On the Origin of Species*
Richard Dawkin's *The Selfish Gene*
Thomas Kuhn's *The Structure of Scientific Revolutions*
Geoffrey Parker's *Global Crisis: War, Climate Change and Catastrophe in the Seventeenth Century*
Mathis Wackernagel & William Rees's *Our Ecological Footprint*

SOCIOLOGY

Michelle Alexander's *The New Jim Crow: Mass Incarceration in the Age of Colorblindness*
Gordon Allport's *The Nature of Prejudice*
Albert Bandura's *Aggression: A Social Learning Analysis*
Hanna Batatu's *The Old Social Classes And The Revolutionary Movements Of Iraq*
Ha-Joon Chang's *Kicking Away the Ladder*
W. E. B. Du Bois's *The Souls of Black Folk*
Émile Durkheim's *On Suicide*
Frantz Fanon's *Black Skin, White Masks*
Frantz Fanon's *The Wretched of the Earth*
Eric Foner's *Reconstruction: America's Unfinished Revolution, 1863-1877*
Eugene Genovese's *Roll, Jordan, Roll: The World the Slaves Made*
Jack Goldstone's *Revolution and Rebellion in the Early Modern World*
Antonio Gramsci's *The Prison Notebooks*
Richard Herrnstein & Charles A Murray's *The Bell Curve: Intelligence and Class Structure in American Life*
Eric Hoffer's *The True Believer: Thoughts on the Nature of Mass Movements*
Jane Jacobs's *The Death and Life of Great American Cities*
Robert Lucas's *Why Doesn't Capital Flow from Rich to Poor Countries?*
Jay Macleod's *Ain't No Makin' It: Aspirations and Attainment in a Low Income Neighborhood*
Elaine May's *Homeward Bound: American Families in the Cold War Era*
Douglas McGregor's *The Human Side of Enterprise*
C. Wright Mills's *The Sociological Imagination*

The Macat Library By Discipline

Thomas Piketty's *Capital in the Twenty-First Century*
Robert D. Putman's *Bowling Alone*
David Riesman's *The Lonely Crowd: A Study of the Changing American Character*
Edward Said's *Orientalism*
Joan Wallach Scott's *Gender and the Politics of History*
Theda Skocpol's *States and Social Revolutions*
Max Weber's *The Protestant Ethic and the Spirit of Capitalism*

THEOLOGY

Augustine's *Confessions*
Benedict's *Rule of St Benedict*
Gustavo Gutiérrez's *A Theology of Liberation*
Carole Hillenbrand's *The Crusades: Islamic Perspectives*
David Hume's *Dialogues Concerning Natural Religion*
Immanuel Kant's *Religion within the Boundaries of Mere Reason*
Ernst Kantorowicz's *The King's Two Bodies: A Study in Medieval Political Theology*
Søren Kierkegaard's *The Sickness Unto Death*
C. S. Lewis's *The Abolition of Man*
Saba Mahmood's *The Politics of Piety: The Islamic Revival and the Feminist Subject*
Baruch Spinoza's *Ethics*
Keith Thomas's *Religion and the Decline of Magic*

COMING SOON

Chris Argyris's *The Individual and the Organisation*
Seyla Benhabib's *The Rights of Others*
Walter Benjamin's *The Work Of Art in the Age of Mechanical Reproduction*
John Berger's *Ways of Seeing*
Pierre Bourdieu's *Outline of a Theory of Practice*
Mary Douglas's *Purity and Danger*
Roland Dworkin's *Taking Rights Seriously*
James G. March's *Exploration and Exploitation in Organisational Learning*
Ikujiro Nonaka's *A Dynamic Theory of Organizational Knowledge Creation*
Griselda Pollock's *Vision and Difference*
Amartya Sen's *Inequality Re-Examined*
Susan Sontag's *On Photography*
Yasser Tabbaa's *The Transformation of Islamic Art*
Ludwig von Mises's *Theory of Money and Credit*

Macat Disciplines

Access the greatest ideas and thinkers across entire disciplines, including

FEMINISM, GENDER AND QUEER STUDIES

Simone De Beauvoir's
The Second Sex

Michel Foucault's
History of Sexuality

Betty Friedan's
The Feminine Mystique

Saba Mahmood's
*The Politics of Piety:
The Islamic Revival and
the Feminist Subject*

Joan Wallach Scott's
*Gender and the
Politics of History*

Mary Wollstonecraft's
*A Vindication of the
Rights of Woman*

Virginia Woolf's
A Room of One's Own

Judith Butler's
Gender Trouble

Macat analyses are available from all good bookshops and libraries.

Access hundreds of analyses through one, multimedia tool.

Macat Disciplines

*Access the greatest ideas and thinkers
across entire disciplines, including*

INEQUALITY

Ha-Joon Chang's, *Kicking Away the Ladder*

David Graeber's, *Debt: The First 5000 Years*

Robert E. Lucas's, *Why Doesn't Capital Flow from
Rich To Poor Countries?*

Thomas Piketty's, *Capital in the Twenty-First Century*

Amartya Sen's, *Inequality Re-Examined*

Mahbub Ul Haq's, *Reflections on Human Development*

Macat analyses are available from all good bookshops and libraries.

Access hundreds of analyses through one, multimedia tool.

Printed in the United States
by Baker & Taylor Publisher Services